Confronting the ruling spirits of Zimbabwe
By Fortunate Hove

1 Kings 18: 21, 24

21 Elijah went before the people and said, "How long will you waver between two opinions? If the Lord is God, follow him; but if Baal is God, follow him."
24 ... The god who answers by fire—he is God."

Chapter	Page
1. Introduction -	6
2. My early life	33
3. Abuse can take many forms	48
4. A child from a broken home	56
5. School and College years	77
6. Training to be an Intercessor	83
7. Separation from my children	107
8. Romance and Destiny	115
9. Careers	127
10. The death of my brother	136
11. My Mandate in California	150
12. Focus on Praying for Zimbabwe	164
13. Powers holding Zimbabwe down	177
14. History and national destiny	194
15. Idolatry	201
16. Deities worshipped in Zimbabwe	212
17. Totems	231
18. The Ruling Spirits of Zimbabwe	240
19. Troubled Marriages	249
20. The Flag of Zimbabwe	265
21. Kurapira/ Protection Rituals	268
22. Rape Victims	271
23. Deliverance	294
24. Testimonies	299
25. Prayer	308
26. A call for Continental African repentance	320
27. Signs of apostasy/ the great falling away	325
28. Conclusion	330
Sources	343

Chapter 1

Introduction

Growing up in the countryside of Zimbabwe, I learned a lot about the cultural norms of my people. The knowledge gained over time helped me in my career later on in life, during which I worked for fourteen years as a journalist and Public Relations Manager.

My decision to write this book was prompted by the desire to give God the glory for protecting me through decades of darkness that shrouded my life. I could not explain what was happening as I endured abuses of all kinds, rejections, and pain. These experiences complicated my life. This was after realizing that what I had been experiencing was very common among girls and women in my culture and other societies. I do not claim to be an authority on spiritual matters, but I have learned many lessons in my mandated divine assignments that I undertook for thirty-three years. I believe that someone will pray for Zimbabwe with renewed vigor after reading some of the passages in this book. Intercessors need to know the raging battle that faces the Zimbabwean woman. I also would appreciate it if the lawmakers could examine the contradiction between traditional beliefs and the Roman-Dutch Law system that Zimbabwe follows. How do you incarcerate a rapist for many years when some traditional structures in place right now, like the installation of chiefs in some parts of the country, encourage orgies and incestuous practices at traditional ceremonies? How do you stop such practices in people's daily lives when they have been formally introduced to such practices by tradition, and they take such practices as a normal part of daily living?

The writing of this book was also born out of years of experiencing adversity in my own life that was heartbreaking.

The whole experience seemed to have been carefully planned.

1. My parents separated when I was very young I was then raised in my mother's family, where I was not welcome.
2. My mother's sister took me into her home. It was a home that one can describe as wealthy by any standard. In that home, my aunt treated me like a

princess. She would dress me up after bathing and then in bright-colored clothes. She would set up a chair just for me and sit me on it. I felt like a princess. I did not know the pain of my own broken family until one day.

3. I was at home with an older child. When I woke up, I discovered that all the adults had left on a shopping trip. I was safe in the house because there were no strangers allowed to enter the house. When I saw an older boy from the village, I rushed back inside the house, I knew that the rule was that no one from the village should enter the house because there was a belief in the family that villagers carried diseases and could be contagious. I knew that I was not like people from the village because they had what I was told was a 'disease' I assimilated into that cultural environment, and it became the foundation of my life. The belief that I am a princess. I deserve better in life. In that atmosphere, the boy from the village followed me inside the house, all the way to my furthest bedroom, and raped me.

4. Rape has no special place of occurrence. My little princess mind was dethroned that day. In my place of safety, a perpetrator found and violated me. My concern in hindsight is that no adult paid attention to the changes that I exhibited soon after. My cousin did not follow into the house to find out what was happening. Something was very bizarre about the circumstances surrounding how I was violated through rape.

With that curiosity, I discovered a system intricately woven into the culture under which my abuse was perpetrated. While the focus is always on the physicality of rape, I realized a spiritual dimension that connected me as a victim. The spiritual aspects under which sexual abuse was carried out related to the environment but tiered from the family unit to the national level. Such a system had many victims. I was not the only victim, as I realized later. The difference is that I talk about it in this book and publicly, yet many were silenced by culture until their death. Others gave up the fight for life because the strength to fight was nipped out of them at a young age, and they never regained their strength.

Another discovery I made is that the abuse of women expressed in many forms is way too common in my nation, regardless of whether people are rich or poor. Although close family members became instruments of my demise, I discovered through relentless searching and prayer that there is a system that has woven itself into a culture that promotes familial abuse, that is spiritual, which manifests in physical expressions.

I was a rape and ritual sacrifice victim, as well as an incestuous sexual assault and pimp victim. It appeared like once I was violated, a gate was opened in my life for other forms of abuse. I did not tell anyone because I was threatened the first time I was raped. I was scared and confused because I did not know what to call the act perpetrated against me. I had been threatened not to tell anyone, and I believed my rapist. I became angry as more abuse was unleashed on me in other forms. I remained quiet, hoping that one day I would escape it all, but that day took decades. I believe that I was born an optimist with the ability to smile. Still, behind all the positive exhibits of my personality, I questioned why I was a target of hate, abuse, rejection, and pain. Some of the painful experiences of my life are hard to justify.

Over time, I have realized that this is the cry and dilemma of rape, molestation, incest, sodomy, and ritual sacrifice victims and that their voices should be heard. That their story is told, gory as the details may be, and that a stop should be put to some traditional beliefs and practices that open up people's lives to destruction.

The act of rape is to force someone to have sex when they are unwilling, using violence or threatening behavior (Cambridge Dictionary). The victim may be groomed first by the perpetrator, threatened, assaulted, and verbally demeaned. My subjective definition is that rape is an act of violation that pollutes a person's destiny.

Reasons for rape are varied. Among the perpetrators are narcissists, insecure men, bullies, and perverts. While lack of self-control is a major motivation for rape, it also appears that the act has a relationship with greed,. Some people desire to be rich, acquire power, and increase production yields in agriculture, using any perverted means they can employ. One of the major beliefs is that a woman can be used to boost all the above because she is a system that reproduces, nurtures, and multiplies. Psychological issues cause people to abuse the weak too. There is a desire for power, wealth, fame, and fortune, which circumvents the principle of hard work and its rewards. For the love of power, fame, farming success, military, and hunting prowess, as well as business excellence, families have subjected themselves to untold suffering in a quest to outdo each other from generation to generation. Some of the challenges I am talking about in this book have been part of our society for ages. Instead of pointing fingers at some individuals, there should be concerted efforts to find a way out of the dilemma. However, I use my experience as an example.

 For some families, their very source of power and influence is the inability of their daughters to have stable marriages. Such families have altars on which the daughters were used as transaction tools for power with the kingdom of darkness. Society sees unmarried women in a family from generation to generation, and no one can comprehend the source of the problem. It is also important to know that when rape has been incorporated as part of a ritual in a family for any intended goal, it becomes institutionalized in that family as part and parcel of worship. Take, for instance, the ancient world, where there was little civilization. The definition of success lay in the ability to hunt, fight, dance, and stone smithing, to mention a few. An individual from a family may have wanted to succeed in battle or hunting. The individual would consult an herbalist who could give them charms that enable them to excel.

    The Book of Enock (2013) sheds light on the origin of herbalism. God was not the source. Fallen angels taught men about herbalism and some of the skills we celebrate today in the name of science and technology. Man, in his fallen nature, was drawn into another level of darkness and rebellion against God by fallen beings. This resulted in more depravity which sought to perpetuate everything that God did not condone in humans created in His image. Military regiments engaged in rituals believed to bring success in battle, but the effects of such engagements outlived the initiators for generations after them. As part of the acquisition of power, there are dos and don'ts that the recipient of the herbs is supposed to follow. An agreement is reached about what to do to sustain the power. In Ndebele, this is called *'intebe'*, where a man gets herbs to strengthen himself. At face value, the act looks innocent because no one disputes the need for self-protection for an individual, especially a man. The herbalist who is consulted is a representative of the fallen angels' system that will enforce the power of the charms. Fallen angels are eternally condemned, and they aim to take humanity down to hell with them. Still, the customer who visits the herbalist is unaware of the bigger system behind the powers exhibited by the herbalist. Once an individual voluntarily consults the herbalist, he opens up his life to the system behind herbalism. This is not a system that one can separate from on a whim because there is a complex interaction between humanity and condemned spiritual beings. The main reason these fallen beings seduce human beings into this inordinate relationship that is not sanctioned by God through beliefs in herbalism and other things is that the fallen beings need the bodies of humans to express themselves. The spiritual law of God is that every person who comes into the world does so through the birth canal or birth in general. Only Satan fell like lightning when he came to earth. He has no body of his own as Jesus Christ had, but he needs to manifest his works. Therefore his presence on earth is illegal because it is not sanctioned by God- John 10:1-2, Luke 10:18 The same applies to the fallen angels who need bodies to express themselves on earth to carry out evil.. Humanity is in a dilemma of being targeted for their physical bodies to be used as mediums by the kingdom of darkness. These fallen beings can use animals too.

Once a person is seduced by this system, only the redemptive power of Jesus Christ's blood can ransom the victim from the hold of darkness. Once under the control of evil powers, there is no limit to what a human can do. This is not done with freedom of choice because once someone falls for the bait of Satan, they become his slave who toils under the bondage of Satan. The person lives to fulfill the demands of the kingdom of Satan. Satan claims such a person as his property or slave because he views the person as a rebel against God just like he did when he tried to stage a coup in heaven.

Consequently, when families engage in perversion and inordinate practices, it is only an expression of the kingdom that they belong to. Do not be fooled, it is not tradition. A tradition that teaches anything contrary to the God of heaven is part of a fallen system, and it will take its practitioners to the lake that burns with fire and brimstone.

The charms may work for a while, but after some time, the real enforcers of the charms, who are not the herbalists but the spirits behind him, confront the receiver with demands that may never end. They can ask for the blood of one of the relatives or the recipient of the charms to offer his children up to the spirits. Usually, the individual accepts the request without knowing that the agreement made is as good as offering his family up to Satan. Therefore, things begin to happen to children, like nightmares, promiscuity, rebellion, and even death. From then on, the family becomes slaves to the spirits that the father or mother consulted through the herbalist for charms. This is the genesis of what is called a generational curse. Once that door is opened, there are spirits of hell that are assigned to enforce the control of the family, which are called watcher spirits. They ensure that everyone born into that family afterward conforms to their mandate on the family. They can ensure that in every generation, one person does not marry. If there are any marriages, they only last a certain number of years, then the spouse dies or the couple divorces. There could be children born with physical deformities. The family comes together occasionally for traditional worship, but they bow down to the spirits that entered an agreement with the founder of that family line. In some families, the women remain in marriages only if they are in control. They are groomed to subvert the order of God of the man being a priest of a house. Such a position of power by a woman perverts the children of the marriage, and the spiral goes on.

    An altar is set up in the family where people gather to worship. It is important to note that some individuals are altars of their families. Everyone in the family listens to the person and obeys. The person is feared. Other family members venerate such a person because he or she is the source of their wealth, and they will everything not to upset such an order that brings wealth.

Apart from people being used as an altar, the round hut called the kitchen in many homes in Zimbabwe doubles up as an altar of worship. This is the kitchen where food is cooked; it is the gathering for all family members for meals, and at times used for formal family meetings. During worship in front of the hut, libations are made, as well as engaging the spirits of the dead. The hut is the best choice for an altar because no one escapes its influence. After all, that is where food is cooked. All the members of the family eat food prepared at the altar called the kitchen. This is why it is difficult for many people to escape familial bondages because the set-up of the homestead promotes the control of the kitchen on every family member. Other huts serve as bedrooms for different family members, but they may exert less influence than the kitchen.

    I lacked understanding and clarity on some of the experiences I went through because my encounters were at a very young age. I can say one thing with certainty, though, the hand of God was upon my life all the way. Otherwise, I would not have lived to write this book. I also realize that, had I not traveled this path, I would not have had any basis to talk about what I have written in the following pages. I am a survivor.

    These are grave issues that are hard to talk about. They are on a tangent with our customs and traditions, in which discussions about sex are taboo, let alone issues of domestic or familial rape. Yet, individuals are suffering quietly behind these traditional taboos. I have found some cultural beliefs very hypocritical, if not outright lies. As a result, many victims cannot talk about their predicament because ' there are issues that cannot and should not be discussed because they destabilize family relations' Family ties in many families have been held together at the expense of untold suffering among the weak, through different forms of abuse.

What has surprised me in my journey as a victim and later survivor of physical, sexual, and ritual sacrifice abuse is that such acts have both a physical, as well as a spiritual nature to them. The physical being the act of violation of the individual's privacy through rape, molestation, incest, and sodomy. Physical violation is also the act of subjecting a defenseless person to pain as punishment or verbal attacks to demean the victim before an assault. My father wanted to excel in business, and to do so, he wanted me to be the sacrifice that would sustain the business. He did not seem to believe in the tenets of hard work. He was a teacher by profession but had some business on the side.

    The spiritual nature of the violation is what I found to be darker than what many people may like to believe. Domestic sexual abuse is connected to the appeasement of spirits, whether familial or national. It is not every woman who is targeted for abuse, though. Victims of this type of violation seem to be carefully selected for that purpose, being individuals with abilities that are natural, like good looks, intelligence as well as birth order. First and last-born children, as well as only daughters in families, are often prime targets for particular types of ritual sacrifices. Other children become victims because of the familial system that subjects a particular bloodline to curses that emanate from previous agreements, breaking of covenants, and murder of innocent people committed by previous generations. Usually, parents are the major perpetrators of such violations. There appears to be a connection with an individual's destiny, physical attributes, and bloodline from which they come.

However, in the case of Zimbabwe, there are not many people excluded from one form of spiritual violation or another. Rape or sexual abuse tops the list of activities relating to abuse many individuals experience for spiritual reasons. The quest for power, wealth, and influence is a major cause of some of the rape cases that innocent people have had to endure in Zimbabwe. This is fueled by a traditional belief system among the tribes of Zimbabwe that for a king or chief to rule, he has to engage in an inordinate sexual encounter with a relative, a young virgin, or even murder a woman ritually. Not only that, but sex can also be used as a weapon to initiate women into a life of bondage where they lose the ability to move on after having sex with certain types of men. Some women die after sexual encounters with men who are not "looking for sex for pleasure" but as a business venture in which either the woman who is the sexual partner dies or she goes on to initiate other men who have sex with her in the future.

In ritual sex, the man who initiates the woman during a sexual encounter does not use sex for pleasure but as a weapon to subdue individuals who become his slaves. This is done to gain more money, influence, and control of his environment. This practice is not gender-specific. The act is steeped in witchcraft, where the virtues of a woman, namely her ability to reproduce and cause multiplication and her fertility related to monthly period cycles, are highly valued for strengthening the power of business, farming ventures, influence, and control in the practice of witchcraft. It is no surprise that most of the targets are adolescent girls. A girl child is a gold mine in many families and the kingdom of darkness because her virtues enable growth, power, and multiplication of their activities if she is 'harvested' at that prime age. After the sexual act, as the girl grows, so does the power, energy, and strength of the person who tapped into her virtues. It is not a coincidence that girls are prime targets of such heinous activities. There is an exchange of virtue in which the girl suffers while the person who puts her into bondage prospers.

Sugar mamas or cougars go after the younger men because they want to tap into youthful strength. Not for pleasure only, but for ritual purposes sometimes. They harvest the sperm and take it to the marine world under the waters of the rivers, lakes, pools, and even the sea, where they interact with mermaids to get power for success. They manipulate the sperm of their sex partner so that the youthful strength of the young man who has slept with them is harnessed for their prosperity. The old women are willing to pay for such services because they become the winners of the game since they may have control of the young man's life until he dies, or they kill him when he is no longer productive. In the same vein, the young man will sleep with other women and initiate them into the system to which he is a slave because a single act of sexual intercourse caused him to surrender his destiny to a stranger. One can argue that careless sexual behavior is behind many untimely deaths in the nation. Life expectancy has not been reduced by poverty only but also due to a lack of understanding of the consequences of sexual sin, especially the one connected to idolatrous worship. This is a common practice in Zimbabwe because the whole nation worships a mermaid spirit, which historian Aeneas Chigwedere calls a common ancestor of the Shona people. These beliefs and practices shift power dynamics at every level of business, politics, influence, and control as people jostle to acquire power traditionally, trashing the value of business ethics. Men and women are happy to lay down their college degrees and undergo initiation into a system that many views as a better means to an end because education does not seem to be able to stand alone as a source of a comfortable life. Indeed, many of them prosper for a season, but it is a prosperity that is laced with a curse. One day, such a support system may collapse even if the person may have climbed high up the ladder of life. A system that promises individuals success with little sweat turns out to be the person's demise. Moreover, prosperity obtained in such a manner is fleeting. The individual who prospers through this ritualistic system cannot claim to own the wealth. He becomes a slave of the system that initiates him, doing the bidding for his or her initiators. The person loses the essence of his humanity, just like Adam, and Eve in the Garden of Eden. Many can only get into power after these rites of passage, where they sell their souls to underwater or marine spirits in exchange for power. political influence, fame, or success in farming. Such a transaction is made by one person, but in time, the marine spirits will begin to demand more from the person if they want to stay in or increase their power. This can come in the form of the desecration of virgins, incest, acts of sodomy, or any weird activity that contradicts what is written in the Bible because the primary aim of marine spirits is to mock God, who ordained sex as sacred. Some victims have their breasts sucked on in the night by unseen forces. Sucking breasts is also a sexual act, but in the case of ritual acts, it serves to suck virtue out of the victim. Virtue in this sense is the excellence that every person has that is God endowed. This may vary from person to person. As a result other people envy what others have, and seek to tap into such virtue for their own good. You may ask, how do you identify such people? This is done by what are called demonic star hunters. A woman can have her breasts sucked by unseen beings during her sleep. The suckers could be snakes, alligators or any other evil creature assigned to suck life out of the person until death. For men, their seminal fluid is power. The kingdom of darkness uses casual sex to access the virtue of men. Casual sex is the death -knell of many men. After a short stint with a woman whom they do not know, many men forget about the experience. However, the woman involved may be a mermaid seeking for men to destroy. Other women are satanic agents who know the power of manhood or womanhood which many people do not know. A woman nourishes a baby through breastfeeding. From that, the baby grows into a healthy individual. In the same manner, demonic forces of initiation are assigned to divert this virtue in a woman to serve the success of the person who engages in the occult. Satan cannot create anything; therefore, he latches onto what God created in humanity for multiplication, prosperity, and procreation and uses it to reward only those who have made a pact with him. When one looks at it closely, one finds out that the individuals targeted are people who can change their environment through God-given gifts, and Satan does not like such people because real-world changers are those who win souls for the kingdom of God. While individual success is worthy of celebration, much of it only lasts a lifetime, but those who get to know God receive eternal life. Satan goes after those who are slated to be world changers and twists their virtue in any way that he can so that they either die without any knowledge of who they are or their mandate on earth.

Mothers have sex with their sons to appease their marine sponsors. Maids, gardeners and guardians take advantage of minors under their care. It is sad that as educated as many people are in Zimbabwe and many parts of Africa, there is no confidence in the power of education to improve the quality of the life of an individual without the use of charms as well as strong backing from traditional spirits. Evidence of the existence of charms is played out in African movies. This is because, from time immemorial, people engaged in rituals that are still practiced today to gain power and influence. The confidence to stand on education or business acumen seems like it needs to be received by many in our African societies.

It is important to note that other cultures engage in practices that empower them to gain wealth through culture-specific rituals which differ from region to region. For instance, Freemasonry worships Ja-bu-lon, composed of three ancient Middle Eastern gods, Jah, the God of the Jews; Baal, the god of the Phoenicians; and On, an Egyptian god. There are many such groups worldwide. Membership in Freemasonry is according to degrees. To every degree, one surrenders to the lodge, and they pronounce curses on their lives and that of their descendants if they decide to quit membership. Many members believe that as members of a Masonic lodge, they are participating in humanitarian service. I spoke to one member who pretended to have quit membership of the lodge, and he said his membership had saved him from being kicked out of the military during active-duty service. Before the hearing of his case, the lodge taught him what to say and how to walk into the hearing venue. Instead of apologizing for his behavior, he made a gesture, moving his hand across his chest, a sign that his life was sacrificed with blood to the lodge. After the gesture, he said, "Is there any hope for the widow's son?" The guy in charge looked at him and told him to go away without hearing, but the other two soldiers on trial had their service terminated. There are a lot of gains that the person engaging in such rituals reaps for a season because once such a pledge is made, the person closes the hope of redemption, and if they decide to come back to God, the curses that they pronounced on their life usually consume them unto death, but their soul will be saved. In my missionary work, I have encountered descendants of former Freemasonry members. Even though their parents were influential while they lived, the children suffer tremendously under bondages that they cannot understand. Again, greed leads people to join secret societies for gain, but it is an act of idolatry in the eyes of God.

    In Zimbabwe, it is easier for predators to pounce on family members because traditionally, those who are older and have influence are respected without questioning within their families. Consequently, when they rape a family member, the act is covered up by other adults around them. The victim is often vilified for making 'false accusations' if they dare to challenge the violation. In such an atmosphere, the practice continues unabated. Victims often have no recourse because they are young and do not know how to challenge a family system that is against them, and also that the perpetrators have the power er to silence the victim. Many girls and women move on after violation because the system in which they are does not value their word. Of course, there are cases of false accusations, too, caused by greed and envy. These are an infinitesimal fraction of rape cases.

    God emphasizes the importance of sexual purity before marriage, as well as in marriage, because sex has been a weaponized act from Biblical times. Hebrews 13:4 says that "Marriage is honorable among all, and the marriage bed undefiled, but fornicators and adulterers God will judge. Have we ever asked ourselves why we accept adultery as a part of married men's lives in Zimbabwe? Now women have also joined in the game of infidelity. It is because adultery is also a part of the lifestyle of those who worship Baal. Adultery is acceptable as long as the nation bows down to the system of worship currently in place. Even for those who go to church, there are times that the national stronghold requires worship, and men and women of God fall into sexual sin in ways that are hard to explain. It is because they have not separated themselves from a culture that appears to be powerful and good without examining its practices.

In terms of destiny, the Bible sheds some light on that issue in two cases. The birth of Moses, and the birth of Jesus Christ, in which their peers were massacred as part of a government policy in Egypt and Palestine (Exodus 1:15- 18, Matt 2:16-18). How did the rulers know that a deliverer was among the baby boys born then? This is where spiritual or supernatural influence on governments can cause the leaders to make good decisions to preserve life or fail to do so if they are influenced by the Baal system. Governments are influenced by either the power of God or the power of Satan. In the case of the birth of Moses, Pharaoh had the plan to kill all male children of the Israelites so that the Israelites would not grow and outnumber the Egyptians. That sounds like a political move, and the sad story as we know it is that the plan was executed, and many little boys were killed. While the decree was in operation, Moses, the redeemer of the Israelites in Egypt, was born. Although he survived, many of his peers died. This is because what appeared like a political decision was a diabolic plan to thwart the process of the redemption of the Israelites. In Palestine, the birth of Jesus Christ was accompanied by a glorious star interpreted by magicians as representing royalty. With that knowledge, the Magi traveled from a distant land to Jerusalem asking, "Where is He who is born King of the Jews? For we have seen His star in the East, and have come to worship Him" (Matt 2:2) This sheds some light on the fact that the birth of a child has many dynamics that come with it. For example, a star accompanies every child born into the world. From Jesus's example, we understand that the size of a star denotes the importance of a person to their mission on the earth. The value of a person is not in what they accomplish personally while they live, but what they accomplish concerning the plan of God for their life while they live. Since the size of the star signifies the purpose or future status of a baby, Satan aims to usurp the original purpose of God for the child at birth. This is what mothers need to understand that many things take place at a hospital where babies are born.

There are spirits called demonic star hunters, whose assignment is to monitor which hospital where big and brighter stars fall because that is a signal to Satan that an individual is born who is going to cause trouble for his kingdom. Demonic star hunters monitor the cosmos for such developments. Identifying such a baby, they start attacking from birth to abort the purpose. Some babies succumb to crib death as part of such spiritual attacks.

In the Zimbabwean tradition, the rituals that a baby is subjected to for protection at birth open up the child's destiny to demonic oppression. However, it is done in the name of upholding a cultural practice. In most cases, the fate of a child is sealed at birth or within the first six months, as they are offered to spirits in many ways that bring bondage instead of protection.

Having had a personal experience with some of the bondages I mentioned, I decided to write about my experience from childhood. I have ministered to countless victims and survivors of ritualistic sacrifices.

Chapter 2

My early life

I was born at Mnene Hospital in Mberengwa district of the Midlands Province. My father was from Chivi, then known as Fort Victoria Province. My birth was a miracle because I narrowly escaped abortion. My father was behind it. I was raised by my mother from about four and half until my late teenage years. My father, capable of taking care of me, abandoned me for twelve years until I decided to look for him when Zimbabwe became independent after the war of liberation. Life was tough without a father. Something had happened to my mother after her separation from my father. For some time, she was angry. I saw her giving up the fight in life. She had no support system at all. She was in a home where family members openly disliked her. I watched and experienced sibling rivalry between my mother and her brothers and sisters, including their mother, which still exists today. Watching all the hardships unfold in my mother's family, I had a very strong sense inside of me that I would win in the game of life despite what was going on around me as early as four years old. I had a passionate desire to protect my mother. I realized that my mother would have to wait until I grew up so that I could take care of her. I cannot explain how I knew about my future enough to have that kind of hope, but I knew later that it was the God of heaven protecting me. I seemed to have a long-range vision that made me see farther than where I was, and I had inside of me what appeared to be a voice of assurance that I would be all right regardless of what I was going through. I had witnessed my father say his last words before the court session at the Chief's homestead as he separated from my mother, my sister, and me. My father said to my mother and the relatives at the session, " I do not need the children, " referring to my sister and me. You can have them as your bonus." I do not recall that part of the meeting because I was only four. I only remember the journey to the meeting.

My mother later told me that when my father uttered those words, I looked at him and broke down crying before the gathering. My crying touched all the adults present, and the chief said to my father, "Young man, how do you feel about the crying of your daughter because you are rejecting her?" In response, my father, unperturbed from what I heard, said, "I speak my mind." With those words, my father left us and never turned back. That was not the last time that my father rejected me. He did it again later on in life. Over the years, my mother kept telling me that I was not an ordinary child. I did not know what the essence of such a statement would mean in my life, but I was a motivated child from a very young age, in spite of the difficulties that my environment presented to me.

I just want to point out one thing about communication. When my father uttered the words of rejection, he could have been addressing the people at the gathering as well as the spiritual powers of the area. I will explain later.

The village where I grew up in Mberengwa had many experiences that were both good and bad for an adventurous child like me. There was a good balance of both positive and negative encounters. Some family members loved me, and that was enough to keep me motivated. Positive input from my teachers at school fueled my resolve to live until I could move on from that environment. Other family members expressed their dislike of me through verbal abuse and beatings that were cruel. For instance, an aunt of mine would gather all the children in the home and then call me out of six kids for a beating. I would be the only one receiving the beating. One day she said, "I want you all to see how I beat the child of a sister that I do not like with a scout belt." She lashed me with that belt as I stood defenseless while other children were watching. I was supposed to smile after such a heavy beating or else, I would be beaten again. My little body was swollen, but I was put to work as if nothing had happened.

    One morning, we were in my grandmother's kitchen, getting ready for school. Our porridge was simmering on the fire, and my aunt was ironing our clothes for the day. My grandmother noticed that she had left out my dress which I was supposed to wear to school that day. My grandmother asked my aunt to iron out my green little dress with a lower waist and two pleats in the front. She responded to my grandmother in a way that made me understand what rejection is from that day on. "I will not iron her dress because I hate her mother" my aunt said. Out of shame and a deep feeling of rejection, I broke down crying. I was in grade two. I wondered what my mother had done wrong to warrant that kind of treatment. My grandmother ironed the dress for me. I knew that my mother was not liked by some family members, and in my mind, I was determined to grow up, acquire an education, and care for my mother. Her siblings talked about her negatively all the time in my presence, and that reinforced my determination to make a difference in her life one day.

  The beatings continued until I was about eleven years when one of my uncles would brutalize me with an ox-hide whip for hours for no reason. Then I ran away from home for days because the anguish was too much to bear. I just wandered around the villages, trying to escape and look for my father. I was found after a few days. That action awakened the community about the possibility of abuse in the home, and the beatings stopped. My hope was in the understanding that one day I would leave that home. I had no attachment to anything in the area.

  Spiritually, I had interesting experiences that I now realize were very deep confrontations with spirits from the dark side. I remember when I asked my grandmother to accompany me to the toilet one night. She was too lazy to wake up, so she asked me to open up the door so she could watch me while I walked outside. The trip did not go very far because a bright red fiery light stood before me in the middle of the night. I called my grandmother, and she yelled for me to come back. I did, but I need to remember if I accomplished my bathroom trip. Nobody explained to me what that bright light in motion was. I remember that I had no fear at all.

The second encounter worth mentioning was during the war of liberation when at eleven years, I was sent to a guerilla base with food in the evening in the company of an aunt who had mental health problems. We got lost in the dark and found ourselves in an area of disused emerald mine pits. Suddenly, we roused a tall being in the area, and it gazed at us from its side. It must have been over two meters tall. There was no home nearby, and the moon was coming up. The being looked ashen in the face and was dressed in clothes that I could not describe well because they looked like layered clothes with the appearance of a too too dress shape. After a startled gaze, the being made a gawkish motion that blended it with the tall Msasa trees. We retreated and took another direction in search of the guerilla base until we found it.

Whenever I relate the story to people from the area, they always say, " You should count yourself lucky because bus drivers and other mine prospectors who had an encounter with that being died." The villagers always add that "Those are custodians of the wealth that is on those hills. This area has abundant mineral wealth, but the wealth has its custodians." People in the area seemed to be aware of the existence of another world that interacted with them. They also showed an attitude of not wanting to cause trouble for themselves by interfering with what was going on in the range of hills overlooking them. That has caused a lot of concern in my mind as I ask myself why local people have relinquished ownership of the land, and the mineral wealth that comes with it to spirits. They are poor, yet their environment is endowed with many varieties of precious stones. They have no problem acknowledging that the wealth in their area does not belong to them. It has custodians who seem to be aggressive.

After completing college, I was determined to open up and operate a mine. I got a prospecting license, and managed to peg my own mine. I ran into the same vibes where locals said I had to get permission from local mediums. I found this to be contrary to what God says in His word, and I refused to bow down and closed up the mine. I realized that the disenfranchisement of Zimbabweans was not only political but on a spiritual level too. Villagers lived on top of wealth that they could not exploit freely. In 1987, I had a dream that took me back to that range of hills by a brook that cut across the main road. It was always flowing with a narrow stream of water, with areas that had algae where the water was held between the stones. The sun would make the water in the brook glimmer, especially in winter. In the dream, a beast that appeared like a hyena or a lion wanted to maul me. I was on the other side of the brook, having just crossed it. Suddenly, the beast appeared from across the brook, determined to attack me. I began to backtrack while I faced it, believing, in that dream, that it could not attack me as long as I looked at it in the eyes. After a long walk backward, facing the beast, I began to recite Psalm 91. On hearing the word of God, the beast disappeared. In place of the beast an old man from our village appeared to me, looking distraught about me, and he asked me whether

I realized how my life was in danger.? The only person I met one day at that same spot was my grandfather- my mother's father. When I greeted him, he did not answer but just looked at me until we each moved on. He was older then and I am not sure if he even recognized who I was. Before that encounter, I had not yet come across anyone in the village who had a height that rivaled the giant that I met that night. The issue of transactions with spirits to gain wealth or fame is a very common practice. In Luke 4, we encounter Satan trying to make Jesus Christ, the one who created the world bow down and worship Satan. Satan claimed that the kingdoms of the world were given to him (referring to the fall in the Garden of Eden of Adam, and Eve)

5. And the devil, taking him up into a high mountain, shewed unto him all the world kingdoms in a moment.
6. And the devil said unto him, "All this power will I give thee, and the glory of them: for that is delivered unto me; and to whomsoever, I will I give it."
7. If thou, therefore, wilt worship me, all shall be thine.
8. And Jesus answered and said unto him, Get thee behind me, Satan: for it is written, Thou shalt worship the Lord thy God, and him only shalt thou serve.

Since the fall of humanity, wealth has been no longer a right for many. Still, an item for transaction with the kingdom of darkness, and many have sold their souls, or the souls of their loved ones, to get what God freely gave to them at the beginning of time and creation, and when they lost it, Jesus Christ came to restore that right. However, it appears that many people are ignorant of the real purpose of restoring the dominion that Jesus Crist came for. In that ignorance, they perpetuate age-old bondage in which humanity is always on the losing side. This is a transaction that my father put me through so that he would be called a wealthy man. He was a trained teacher who could have made a decent living out of his career, but he chose to destroy my life to get wealth. He is not the only one. In many families in Zimbabwe, girl children are not respected at all. They are dispensable. They can be used as the merchandise that profits other family members. My father, under pressure from some of his relatives to justify why he was destroying my life, was quick to say that he did not care about daughters because his true children were his sons. Many people engage in this practice to succeed in their time. However, this kind of success is phony. Thank God for grace. Otherwise, I would have been physically sacrificed at some point at the altar of wealth. I am not the only one in Zimbabwe who has suffered in that manner. There are many, both living and dead, who have perished without fulfilling their destinies because someone decided that they are not worthy of living their lives freely.

From 2003, I was in the United States, engaged in heavy intercession. Whenever I prayed against environmental spirits, I would have a series of dreams that took me back to the range of hills that overlooked our village. Strangely, the hills did not only abound with vegetation but there appeared to be a community of people not visible to the eye that was thriving in that same area, with high-rise buildings, cars driving around, and even a graveyard of about two hundred people. I was baffled by the dream initially, but whenever I prayed for the area, I would be taken in my dreams to that range of hills. I would see a thriving community with homes and people living in what appeared to be a normal community, but I knew that the area was not settled by any humans. It was a range of hills with natural vegetation. The settlements were subterranean. There was something connected with my demise that was in that range of hills. I did not know what it was. When the dreams about the area intensified, I did some spiritual mapping and realized that the area fell within the vicinity of where my father had rejected me and my sister at the Chief's court.

Then the words of my father that he was said to have uttered revived in my mind. Through grace and an act of spiritual intelligence, I understood that when my father was giving us away as a bonus to my mother, and the community, he was also giving us over to the spirits of the area as their bonus. How does one get a bonus? It is a reward for performance beyond expectation. I understood that my father had offered us to strange spirits for power, and he did not care to respect my mother's family at all because, as far as he was concerned, he was dealing with superior beings. My father believed that he had sealed our destiny through open rejection. That rejection was strong around me. I endured many things behind that rejection from a father. Then one day, I dreamt being taken to that area. Still, I fought to scale up to the top of the hill from the subterranean community, driving a car over stones and boulders as I went up almost vertically along the hill until I came to a plateau where I could see the land of the living in all directions. Then I declared my freedom and that of my children. I had no idea what freedom that was. I learned later that it was a rejection of my father at four during a traditional court session. I am not sure of what else had happened in that area, but something kept bringing me back to that area in dreams. The rejection by my father had opened my young life to bondage that left my destiny stuck in the range of hills. The hill range was close to the chief's home. I do not believe my father ever dreamt of me regaining my freedom, but I did in Jesus Christ.

When an authority figure rejects a child, Satan contends for the child because a spiritual law of Covering by an Authority figure would have been violated. Authority figures in a person's life are not for window dressing. They play a major role in safeguarding the physical, and spiritual well-being of a child. The covering of a child is the parents. They guide the child in a foundational way that gives them the apparatus needed to navigate the meanders of life. When parents love a child, the love is communicated to the core of their being, the spirit. That communication creates safety, confidence, and hope in a child. The absence of those qualities means a child develops a void in their personality. That void is not left vacant for long. Gloom, hopelessness, and loneliness take over. These undesirable qualities can cause observers to predict failure in a child because they see the absence of positivity. For instance, at school, we have a principal. The words that he speaks to children at a young age stick in their minds for a long time, whether they be positive or negative. That is why we find that some people cannot shake off the words that were pronounced over them by their teachers. This is because an authority figure failed to be a covering and became a door opener to the child's destiny through negative words. The negative words and the force that follows them begin to drive the destiny of a child in the wrong direction. Very often, the words will seek to redefine the encoding that is in the star of the child in a bid to enslave the person. Such curses usher in low self-esteem and confusion in a person. After many years, my destiny was still contested in the area where my father gave me away, thereby abdicating his role as my covering. I had to fight with the guidance of God to escape from that hold of darkness through prayer. Once, I drove up that hill like a mad woman with determination, as there was no road, but rocks were strewn all over, I won the battle against obscurity in my life. Although

I may never know what was in that place, my prayers kept bringing me back to the range of hills. I remember standing on that plateau, celebrating my emergence from a strange place, as I felt and celebrating my freedom; I never had that dream again to this day. I look at what it took to emerge from such hidden bondage, and I ask myself how many people are determined to fight for their destiny until they win. In those moments, I fall to my knees, and I give God the glory. Who am I that He would guide me to victory over serious childhood bondages?

Chapter 3
Abuse can take many forms

In my second grade, my guardians said that they could no longer stay with me, and they sent me back to my mother and grandmother, and my place was taken over by another female cousin.

Heaven knows what happened to her, too. Before I came to that home, there was an older girl, whom I always found crying in her room, and I wondered why she was crying so desperately. The home was full of all the comforts that children dream of but in the midst of all that the teenager was always crying. There was an uncaring accusation levelled against her. Some family members said that she had numerous boyfriends and that her ways were crooked regarding her relationship with men. She would cry whenever she had space to be alone or in my company. She had been brought into the family from her home far away from the area before I came in. Hers, were the desperate cries of a young girl whose life was in trouble. For some reason, she was always crying even in the midst of plenty. Hers was the anguish of the soul. When she left for boarding school, I came in to take her place. My own family was broken. The extended family came in to rescue the situation and took me in. Sounds like an innocent thing for a family to do in caring for children of relatives, but there was more to it. The girl children who were relatives served a purpose in the home, which appeared very rich by all standards of the 60s and 70s. Am I disparaging wealthy people? By no means! My experience was one of servicing an altar of wealth and fame, and when my services were done, I was moved out, and another victim came in, and relatives stopped coming when girl children were born to the family. As a child, I would hear conversations in which issues sacred artefacts in the family, and how disputes arose over how they were to be kept.

When I came back to my grandparent's home, my uncles came after me, wanting to have sex with me. One raped me when my grandmother was away. The environment was very different. There was poverty and very little care for younger people in the family. From that, I learned how to care for others due to the neglect I saw and experienced in that home. This was a different altar of darkness, too, serviced through incestuous sex, so it manifested its control of the environment by coming after me. It was like I was a child marked for destruction. Ever wondered how pedophiles and human sex traffickers target their victims? There are outward and spiritual identifying markers for people who get victimized. Outwardly, there can be exhibiting characteristics that attract perpetrators. There are also invisible markers that are put on people which identify them in the spirit realm, according to the ordinances that have jurisdiction over them, as mentioned in Colossians 2:14-15, *14 Blotting out the handwriting of ordinances that was against us, which was contrary to us, and took it out of the way, nailing it to his cross; 15 And having spoiled principalities and powers, he made a shew of them openly, triumphing over them.* Only Christ can change that identity because it is only His blood that is pure enough to erase the identity put on a person by darkness.

All these acts are part of the worship system that forms the culture of Zimbabwe. These altars thrive on the blood or desecration of innocent boys and girls, some of whom grow up as prostitutes, drug addicts, and failures, and we all frown at them. One night, my mother and grandmother were not home, and a second uncle came to spend the night pretending that he was taking care of us, yet he had plans to have sex with me. I resisted him all night. I was in grade four. After he failed to have sex with me, he said, "I am going to find you a boyfriend. You are mature enough to have a boyfriend" He found the boyfriend, and brought him to me. In doing so my uncle was pimping me. Sex trafficking is going on, daily in villages, cities, regions, countries, subregions, continents, and the rest of the world. My mother saw a letter that the pimp's boyfriend had written to me and intervened, but she had no idea it was her brother behind it all. At that rate of abuse, I would have been a good-for-nothing girl. I became angry, not wanting anyone to touch me, and was fighting for my freedom, because I had realized that I had been violated before.

One day my mother beat me up mercilessly because she was under pressure from her family to discipline me because they all thought that my behavior was unbecoming. I was a child crying for help, and my mother had no idea why I was acting up. I was seeing the hypocrisy all around me, and my heart got sick from such observations. I challenged that system without fear. That brought so much pressure on my mother, and at one time she had to beat me up to show that she did not condone my behavior. I had nowhere to run to. So, I went and hid in a bush not knowing what else to do because the only person who was supposed to protect me was not perceiving my heart's cry. My mother searched for me and found me with a swollen body, and she began to cry. She apologized, and I reluctantly accepted her gesture of reconciliation. She never beat me up again. After my encounters with my uncles, I then vowed that no man would ever violate me again. This is a good statement, but it was reactionary. Such a stance can be the spawning ground for hardline feminism if not tempered by grace. When feminism is born out of a reactionary attitude to abuse and pain, it spreads many things other than the quest to level the playing field. Reactions can be based on anger, unforgiveness, desire to prove oneself, vengeance, and hatred. It meant that my response to any gesture of love was suspicious at first. I could not just date all and sundry. God, knowing my brokenness, had brought one person who seemed to understand me naturally, but even that failed too. My experience with rape had robbed me of a natural response to love because the men in my life had failed to model anything good before my eyes. Even when God was directing me to that potential suitor, He knew my brokenness, so God took time to endear the person to me until I opened up emotionally. No other man succeeded in appealing to my heart in that manner. This was because trusting men was a challenge. I was hyper-vigilant.

    We are quick to talk about human trafficking at continental or global levels. Still, child sex trafficking for wealth, fame, success in agriculture, political power, and celebrity connected to our belief system that is culturally based remains the elephant in the room, which is not addressed because it is commonplace to the point of being a norm. The victims are expected to gather whatever remains after their desecration and move on as if nothing happened. The so-called unity in families hides a lot of pain among those who have no voice in their families. I have realized that whenever one talks about the injustice they suffered at the hands of family members, they are accused of causing discord.

I have watched my relatives try to change the narrative of what happened to me by hurling every kind of accusation that they can at my mother and me. In their guilt and shame, they have not chosen the path of apology but to accuse, isolate, and hate. This is because many of them did not believe that we would suffer such levels of abuse and still live. They had pronounced death over us in their minds, but somehow we have survived. Their frustration is palpable.

One realizes that the worship of a Nephilim is also trying to subjugate people to the point of being estranged from their families. The love that is espoused by the Bible has become a meaningless issue in the face of a desire to sacrifice other human beings at the altar of Mulimo. The cruelty of Satan, seeking to destroy the family unit through greed and envy, has gripped the land of Zimbabwe for centuries. Sad, as things were around us, I saw the power of forgiveness in my mother. I worried at some point that my mother could suffer from Stockholm Syndrome because the more she was abused, the more she loved. I struggled for a while with rejection, especially from my father, because I realized that no matter how much I loved him, I had realized that if someone fights you from conception and abandons you when you are born. You look for him when it should be the other way round, and when you find him, then he tries to manipulate your destiny again without mercy, then you face the chilling reality that the only person that they called 'dad' never wanted them. How do you process the grief that comes from such a reality?

Chapter 4

A child from a broken home

In my late teens, I went to live with my father, who was married, and had another family. Zimbabwe was independent, and families could reunite. Relations with my mother's sisters had not gotten any better. I lived with my aunts as a day scholar in town. My mother could not afford boarding school. I would be woken up at 3 or 4 A.M to clean up the house, prepare breakfast for everyone in the house, and after that would I prepare for school, which was some walking distance to make it in time for assembly at 7 A.M. I lived the life of being accused as a prostitute by one of my aunts. I had no boyfriend, but she labeled me a prostitute day and night.

I enjoyed going to church for bible study in the evenings. Whenever I returned home, I found the house locked. I was prepared to sleep outside because I loved Jesus Christ, and nothing could stop me from attending church.

However, I realized it was a matter of time before I was banished from my aunt's home. I was concerned that my aunt was determined to make me stop going to school. I decided to contact my father in the third term of Form one. The war had broken any possibility of communication between me and my father. I had to make a quick decision because I would likely stop attending school. At least my father had a duty to send me to school even if he had abandoned me I had no one else to help me. One of my uncles had told me plainly, "No one is going to help you with school fees because you have a father." I wrote my father a letter using the old address he had used before the war, and he got my letter. After receiving my letter, my father quickly responded by sending me $180. It was a lot of money then. My uncle took it all and never shared a dime with me except for paying the $30 school fees for the term. I communicated with my father, and we both agreed I should move to Hurungwe, where he worked. It would be another year before I could move. I had decided to complete my Form Two at the same school and then move. I told my mother about my plans, and she said to me, "You can go now because you are mature enough to survive any challenges" I did not tell my uncle or my aunts that I was leaving for Karoi. Only my mother knew.

I am my father's oldest child. I struggled to call him dad. Our relationship was never good enough for me to call him dad. I was not used to that. I would say "Good morning" and not acknowledge who he was. I was a stranger to him and his family. He had to demand that I call him dad. Then it sank into my mind that perhaps it was courteous to salute him like that. He had other children with his wife and another daughter soon after I was born with another woman. I immediately saw a dilemma in my half-brother, who, before my arrival, was known as the firstborn. Suddenly there was a girl who was said to be the legitimate firstborn. Not only that, there were two more girls older than him. The three older girls were the ones who were official, nobody was sure how many children had been born after me before the boy. My father was a playboy. He had many children, some of whom looked like us who were official, bearing a strong resemblance to people who were strangers. There are known cases of such siblings, but they officially belong to other families.

Back to the story of the attempted abortion of my pregnancy. My father married my mother in line with the normal process of traditional marriage, and when they would have had a wedding, things fell apart at the last minute. My mother had no support from her family. She was a black sheep in denial. She tried to fit into her family, but instead of the family supporting her marriage, they pulled the rug from under her feet. Yet, traditional expectations required her to honor the same people who did not care for her. When my mother was pregnant with me, one day, my father gave her a pill. He explained that it was to strengthen the pregnancy, but through a workmate, my mother discovered that the pill was to induce abortion. Through the intervention of my mother's workmate, I survived the abortion. My mother did not tell me the story, and I overheard her talking to a family member as if it were a casual issue. I forgave my father because I thought it was part of his youthful folly.

During my stay with my father, I realized that his plans for me were not noble at all. On my 21st birthday, I wanted to go to a nearby game park to have a braai with my family, to celebrate my birthday. My wish was accepted by my father, and when we were making plans for the trip, I realized that it was a group of about four men only, and I would be the only female. I wondered why it was a trip composed of men for a girl's birthday, leaving behind my siblings or the men's wives. As we were getting ready, an elderly woman from a local village died, and the trip was canceled. My birthday was not celebrated at all after the announcement of a funeral. That left me baffled.

I had many conversations with my father that touched on politics, dating, education, and the most heated discussion was always about my faith. He seemed at a loss because I was so committed to my faith, yet I did not lack anything in this life. So, he thought. I owe God every breath because He preserved me when my father's money was not there. My father would often sigh and say, "Why were you not made a boy? You are a loving, caring person. You are a natural leader. The man you are going to marry has it made. I am the one who will suffer loss. If only you were a man, then I would be set"

My stepmother would tell me the story of Catherine the Shrew. She would say, "Catherine the Shrew will be tamed one day." I loved my stepmother very much because from what I had heard about my father's personality, I saluted her for staying with him in the marriage. I could still see signs while I lived with them that they fought over my presence in the home. I did not want my father to go through a second failed marriage, so I was determined to be a good girl in every sense of the word. There was never a time that I talked back to my stepmother. I am a very independent person, and because of my distrust of people due to my earlier experiences in life, I did not allow anyone into the core of who I am. I guarded my personality and protected my independence. I was surprised to hear local people ask me how I managed to live in such a home. I dismissed them as a prying lot, desiring to find some juicy gossip to fuel the community rumor mill. I did not entertain outside interference in the affairs of my family because I believed in the power of prayer.

My stepmother gave me a name. It was more of a title, "Huruyadzo- Biggest one" As the oldest child, I thought that the title referred to my position as the oldest child. Besides that, I was also chubby. I dismissed it initially when she gave me that name. Still, on further investigation, I discovered that it was a shortcut for "Huruyadzo Pfambi- Biggest prostitute"

Unfortunately, my lifestyle was the opposite of the wish of that name or title. I was determined to live a clean lifestyle as a follower of Christ. I did not even have a boyfriend, but word soon spread that I was not only a prostitute but a witch as well. It was so bad that I would meet supposed family friends, and when I greeted them, they would run away from me out of fear that I would hurt them. I was oblivious to all the blackmail coming from our household. When blackmail failed, my father started insinuating that I didn't need to marry, but my sister was free to do so. I asked him why? He responded that I was too intelligent for him to lose me to another man. It was a casual statement, but words that carry bondage in them are often in a somewhat casual manner. I knew he was serious, which grossed me out because my father envied my natural gifts, wanted them for himself and did not care about me. Later on, my stepmother came to me and gleefully said, "I did not give birth to a daughter in this family. Therefore no girl in this family is going to get married." Again, I asked her why, and she just laughed. My father realized that it was not easy for him to make me do anything contrary to the will of God with success. He asked me to leave a Pentecostal church and join the Catholic church, which he claimed to be the official family church. My experience in the family did not give me any incentive to join the Catholic church. I remain Pentecostal to this day. My father realized that I dismissed everything that he tried to say in a bid to harness me into his plans, so he decided to use my stepmother. She came to me and said, "You are not supposed to marry. We have plans for you to stay here and be a spirit medium of your dead grandmother." I laughed at that. She was very serious.

What she did not know was that soon after I was born again, I had a vision of my maternal grandmother introducing me to a woman who was said to be my father's dead mom. My maternal grandmother said, "Your dead paternal grandmother wants you to be her spirit medium." I responded with a song because I did not know any bible verses then. I remember looking at the woman and pointing my finger at her, and saying, *"I command you, Satan, in the name of the Lord, to pick up your weapons and flee. For the Lord has given me the authority to walk all over you"* Immediately, the dead grandmother responded by saying, "Mwana wacho an open a" handingagari"- the child is shining bright, and I cannot stay" She ran away. In other words, if I

63

had accepted her in my dream, then she would have come with darkness in my life, but thank God that I had the light of Christ shining in me by then. Many people are initiated into the kingdom of darkness through dreams. Dreams are a form of communication. That is why Jesus Christ's life was saved because Joseph was told by God in a dream to take the young child to Egypt. I won the victory over an ancestral demon in my dream, masquerading as my dead grandmother. When my stepmother brought up the case again, I realized that the issue of the dead grandmother was at the center of what they intended to do with my life, which was a ritual sacrifice of me for their business. The business was a general dealer store with a grinding mill and an outlet for an opaque brew. Later on, a bottle store was added to the business.

While I was with my mother, my father still harbored the idea of performing that ritual, so he tried the initiation through dreams, but that also boomeranged. When family members want to sacrifice us, they soften us by using familiar names. My dead grandmother had nothing to do with what was going on, but her name was a cover-up for a strange spirit that my parents wanted to put on me. By pronouncing that no girl child would be married in our entire family, my stepmother made me realize that someone was responsible for initiating such an outcome. My father and stepmother had no idea that I knew of the darkness surrounding the so-called spirit of the grandmother and that I had defeated it by the power of God. However, that disclosure of their plans was followed by a very difficult season in my life. I remember, one afternoon, while I sat on the bus passing by Mbare Studios, I had an open vision of a man who looked familiar, but he walked straight into me. It was a strange thing happening while I was riding the bus from the City Center to Glenview. I remember asking my pastor what that meant, and without knowing who it was, I quickly deferred to our Pentecostal beliefs that God was showing me a man who would be a possible suitor. Both my pastor and I were deceived on that issue.

There were also signs of moral decadence in the house. One day, a college student from the area visited our home in the evening. It was strange for him to plan on spending the night at our house without any forewarning. He showed up around dusk on a bicycle. My father, stepmother, and I had to entertain him before we retired to bed. The young man was somehow connected to my stepmother's family, but they had never met before until that evening. In the course of our conversation, my stepmother jumped on the lap of the young man. While we were all dumbfounded by the act, my stepmother jumped back to her seat. We continued the conversation as if nothing had happened while still wondering if what we had just witnessed was real. The young man did not comment on the issue soon after. Later, he said, "I came to your home to see if what I had heard about you was true. My sister-in-law heard your stepmother asking for prayers at a women's meeting, saying that you are a witch and that without divine intervention, she may die at your hands. When I came to your home that evening, my family was very worried because they thought that I was going to spend the night in a dangerous environment. You need to know that everyone who goes to that church believes that you are a witch determined to kill your stepmother. I came to your place against the advice of my family, and I must say there was something that baffled me. Why did your mother throw herself on my lap? She did not know me! It was very daring of her to throw herself onto the lap of a stranger right before her husband" I felt very small before the young man.

A similar story happened during my marriage proceedings. The Munyai/mediator went home to discuss the way forward with the marriage process. The Munyai returned angrily, and he quipped, "You have an amazing family. I have never seen people who are as free as those people. Do you know that your mother tried to hit on me? She only stopped when she realized that we share the same totem. Then suddenly, I became her brother. It was a mess, but those are your people." How do you defend such behavior from the person who should receive the highest honor and respect during the marriage ceremony of a daughter? The Munyai/mediator was related to the family I was marrying.

The worst experience for me was when my stepmother came to me and said, "Just be careful because your father wants to have sex with you" In absolute shock, I looked at my stepmother and asked why? She just said that she was giving me a heads-up. Then she went to my father and said, ``Your daughter told me you want to sleep with her." My father was very angry with me and struggled to talk to me for a long time. I did not know why my father was acting out until one of the family friends told me to stop coming home and then disclosed why my father was upset with me. I was a good Christian girl, trying, by all means, to preserve myself for my future husband because I knew I would have some explanation to give on my wedding night as a rape victim. Then to imagine that the people who were supposed to be my guardians entertained the thought of abusing me in that manner left me very bewildered. I went to tell my mother, who at that time could hardly do anything about my situation. She was concerned but not surprised because she said that she knew that my father was up to no good from the days she was with him. I could see so much worry on my mother's face, and she could only caution me to be careful.

This is not surprising when one understands the connection between the worship of ancestral spirits, Mulimo, Nehanda, and all the other deities, that any form of worship directed at them has to carry an element of vileness, and indiscreet sexual encounters characterize the lives of people who have erected such places of worship in their environment. These places of worship or altars speak. Their language may not be similar to our dialects, but they speak languages that range from inordinate sex, shedding innocent blood, defiling of virgins, sodomy, and strife. You find the lives of people in a particular family being taken out at the same time year in and year out. In some families, every male has to taste living in prison or murdering people. These altars, which are built initially for success, are the one element that is responsible for stagnation and confusion in Zimbabwe, and they start at the family level. Discretion in sexual preferences is out of the question when people worship on these altars, calling it *chivanhu - tradition* because the altars are there to mock God. They mock God through the actions of their captives. No one ever went to a witch doctor to be empowered to become a sexual pervert. No! They will be in search of making their lives better without waiting on God by learning His principles. Then sooner or later, they realize that they would have not only surrendered their destiny to strangers, but they would have brought their family under a curse. A curse that may inflict on coming generations unless mercy is sought through Jesus Christ. When Christ is invited into such an environment, He comes and does the same thing he did in the temple, where he turned the tables of money changers. In Matthew 21:12

Then, Jesus entered the temple courts and drove out all who were buying and selling there. He overturned the tables of the money changers and the seats of those selling doves. Jesus Christ wants to come into a life captured by false worship and kick out those who are usurping the purpose and destiny of the individual. He alone knows how to kick out strongholds from your life.

One witch doctor after another came to our home, and I had no idea what their mission was, but the struggles in my life made me realize that something was after my life. I would be shown by the Holy Spirit the times when my father consulted witch doctors in different parts of the country. I would know exactly where he was and then pray against it. I became afraid of our home and my parents, but there was no other father that I could run to. Without realizing it, you lose faith in institutions that are said to be pillars of society because as far as you are concerned those pillars fight everything that you stand for. You lose faith in humanity, and that is the lowest place that any individual can find him or herself. You fight to survive daily, but you sense an invisible net closing in on you, and you are not sure whether to run or stay put. I told one doctor my problem, and he prescribed what I later came to know that it was anxiety medication. I cannot describe the feeling of calmness and freedom I experienced after taking that pill. I returned for another prescription, and he said, "No." Without realizing it, I would have been hooked on prescription medication, but my doctor saw through it and stopped me at that stage. This is the beauty of the ethical medical practice I experienced with most doctors in Zimbabwe. In such an atmosphere of confusion, my stepmother took me to our general dealer store, where there was a grocery store, bottle store, and grinding mill, and she showed me the safe for money. There was no money in it. Instead, there was a creature that looked like an octopus with many legs. She said, "This is what is keeping us in business." I didn't say a word. From that time, the battle for me to survive as a Christian began. The Holy Spirit came to me, and said, *"You need to gradually withdraw from this family. You have been healed from the abandonment of your father, and he has been healed by your presence in His life. Now is the time to move on."* Then the Holy Spirit came to me again with an issue that amazed me, *"You see that the money from this business is not clean. How do you accept that money?"* The Holy Spirit warned me not to partake of that money. He asked me to bring all the

money to Him, and then he directed me to give the money to my local pastor and other needy people. I would remain without money, although I had brought lots of it from home during my high school days at a boarding school. The Holy Spirit then told me, "I will teach you how to live by faith" The idea was to dissociate me from the contamination of the money from my household. Some of us enjoy cursed money without asking God how to live in environments where we know that idolatry is practiced and most of the wealth in the home is cursed, yet we call ourselves Christians. What do you expect God to do when He judges those who partook in idolatrous ways?
You will be included in the judgment because Satan claims you as his own since money dedicated to him is what sustains you. He is your master. There is a great need for believers to know how to avoid touching an unclean thing. I only knew about it when the Holy Spirit pointed it out to me, otherwise I would not have acted any differently. Many of us succumb to curses that bind our families because we never think of the importance of sanctification- being set apart for the Lord. In that state, you avoid all things that God disapproves of. This is not only abstaining from adultery and

fornication but avoiding money acquired by dubious means. If we enjoy the spoils of wickedness, then we should not expect our lives to be trouble-free because we have not separated ourselves from that which is evil. The wealth that some families enjoy is dedicated to evil powers, and as such, the children from such families have to know that they cannot enjoy the spoils without suffering the consequences of the works of their parents. When a business, project, or office of authority is dedicated to the devil, then expect that the person responsible for doing such a thing cannot leave any legacy in any way. If it is wealth, it also disappears when the person dies, and the same goes for any project or livestock. This is because the moment the person is moved by greed or envy into looking for extra powers and acquires them from the kingdom of darkness, the process of initiation is undertaken. When that process is done, then the person no longer has any power over the affairs of their life because the initiation process takes it all away from them, making them or a slave in turn.

The children born to such families, whatever they gather, or the legacy they seem to build, do not belong to them; they are the property of their masters. That is why you can count on your fingers the number of families that have wealth that has been passed on from one generation to another in Zimbabwe because most of the people who appeared to be rich were not the owners of the wealth, no matter what they say because, the Nephilim who enter into pacts with the living take over the control of the wealth, and they release it only to those who are willing to surrender their birth rights to them. Wealth is for humans, and it was put in each geographic region by God. The Nephilim do not own anything, but they take the wealth of humans through deception, and they end up owning everything and subjugating humans, who have to negotiate access to that which was freely endowed to them by God. The Nephilim in turn require humans to sell themselves to their authority in exchange for wealth, yet God gave it to humanity as a heritage on earth for free. The ultimate objective of the Nephilim is to produce hybrid humans who do not have the DNA of God, just like the race of Goliath of Gath, Og of Bashan, and Sihon, king of the Amorites. That is why God took away their land and gave it to the Israelites. He did not want that race to multiply, but its remnant survived the flood and is wreaking havoc on

earth in different parts of the world. God gave them time to repent when He talked to Abraham, pointing out that Israel had to wait in Egypt while the race of the giants was being given time to turn from their wickedness. God pointed out in Genesis 15:16 *In the fourth generation they will return here, for the iniquity/cup of the Amorites has not yet reached its full measure."* They tested the patience of God until they reached the full measure of iniquity, resulting in their loss of land. God is no respecter of persons. Zimbabwe needs to reconsider its ways of ancestral worship and veneration of Nehanda and Mulimo because the plight of that nation can only be solved by repentance from sin and a wholesale submission to God. If there is no repentance, then judgment is imminent. Zimbabwe is subject to a worldwide system called Babylon the great, the mother of harlots mentioned in Revelation 18, that has used human greed to bait people into bondage with a likelihood of ending up in eternal separation from God due to idolatry. God put in place principles of prosperity that bring satisfaction, Proverbs 10:22 *The blessing of the Lord, it maketh rich, and he addeth no sorrow with it.*
My father told me that he had visited a bus owner in a bid to research routes that he could

service when he had bought buses. I did not know that he wanted to buy buses. I was worried about his move because I did not trust his business acumen. However, after High School, I started having dreams of visits from a man who would have sex with me in the night. I did not know him. I had no boyfriend at that time. I was very confused by the occasional sexual encounters at night. One day, I had a dream of wearing a wedding ring and had no clue what that meant. Later on, I realized that I had been married to a spirit husband- a mermaid spirit that claims a woman as its wife. It can only do so if it has been given access to the person by an authority figure in their life. I began to struggle to do things that were very natural for me to do. I could see my intelligence waning.

In my second year in college, I nearly lost my mind because I could not sleep in my room. Each time I tried to sleep; a force would attack me as if trying to pull out my heart. I would cry to Jesus Christ, then wake up very tired from the fight. I hardly slept that year, and I developed insomnia. I could not focus on my schoolwork; everything was a struggle. The Lord delivered me from the attack, but I did not do well in some of the examination papers

I had prepared in my room. It was a fight to live soberly because I felt dirty from having sexual relations with someone I did not know. I prayed and got some victory, but for a season.

Chapter 5

School and College years

In 1980, the year of Zimbabwe's independence from British rule, I had a life-changing experience. One afternoon, I accompanied my aunt to the vegetable market. I do not remember our family ever buying vegetables from that market, but on that day, we walked to Kwa Todd market. It was called KwaTodd because the missionary from New Zealand, Sir Garfield, who was based at Dadaya, had built it for vendors. That was my first time going to that market. My aunt took her time picking the bundles of vegetables she liked while I stood idly by with no interest in being at the place. I knew that Sir Todd was at Dadaya and that he had been a Prime Minister of Rhodesia way back before I was born. I had never seen him physically before. Absent-minded, I felt some hands laid on me from the back. In bewilderment, I stood still, frozen. Then I shrugged off the hands from my shoulders. I turned around, and this tall Whiteman with bushy eyebrows towered over me, smiling. I had no clue who he was, but he had deliberately laid his hands on my shoulders. He walked on smiling because he could see that I had been shaken. My aunt told me who he was. "That is Todd, he is a good man" I was relieved that my aunt was not going to ask me complicated questions about why the man had laid his hands on my shoulders if I did not know him. In hindsight, I believed that he was praying for me, but I did not know it. A few weeks later, I gave my life to Jesus Christ. I was born again on October 26, 1980. It was during a school midterm break in Zvishavane.

I was coming back into town from visiting my mother in the village when suddenly I heard the sound of music from nearby. A voice said inside me, *"This is what you have been looking for"* I dumped my bags, greeted the people in the house, then went to the venue of the music hurriedly.

It was a church meeting of a tent crusade by the Apostolic Faith Mission Church. The church had been pioneered by John Graham Lake, an American missionary to South Africa.

By 1980, local people were carrying on the legacy of spreading the good news of the gospel. In their work, they brought the Light of Christ to me. I surrendered to Jesus Christ, and He embraced me forever. This is the wisest decision I have ever made; I owe my very existence today to that decision. From the salvation experience, I was privileged to hear the voice of God. When I say God spoke to me, I mean it. I have heard the voice of God directing me in life, teaching me how to be a good person, guiding me on the best choices to make, as well as showing me questions that would be in examination papers before I write tests. God became a Father to me. He would teach me how to dress well and when to change my wardrobe. I did not sit for interviews like other people for my first two jobs because God sent me into the companies as an emissary to redirect the course of the organizations through prayer. One thing that has never been wanting in all the assignments is persecution. God is a Father to me. I have seen Him go hard after people who persecute me with fury. Yet He instructs me to keep quiet when people fight me because He knows how best to handle them. Remember, I had no authority figure over my life since the day that my father relinquished his fatherhood to me. I had uncles and aunts, but they also had problems accepting me and my sister because our father had rejected us. God needed my cooperation to take over the role of an authority figure. Surrendering my life to Jesus was an act of accepting the total authority of God over my life. This is because God makes it His duty to Father, the fatherless, if He is given a chance to do so by the affected people- *Psalm 27: 10, When my father and my mother forsake me, then the Lord will take me up.*

I believe that the prayer of the elderly Sir Todd softened a teenager who had argued in class a few days before that there is no God into a tender recipient of salvation. I was angry, and no one could tell me in class during the debate that there is a God because I was determined to argue against it. My classmates, who did not know my background, were scared of the stance that I took on the existence of God. Their warnings scared me because I believed they saw a true heathen in me based on what I said. God was waiting patiently at the vegetable market for an encounter with Him through the veteran missionary. Incidentally, four years after my salvation experience, God called me to the mission field of America while

I was in High School. The actualization of the call was exactly at the time of the death of Sir Garfield Todd in 2002. I was packing my bags, getting ready to depart for America in answer to the call of God, when I heard of Sir Todd's death. By that time, I was used to hearing God's voice. God instructed me to go to Dadaya to bury Sir Garfield Todd because I was "*…supposed to pick up something from there*" I obeyed and arrived at Dadaya during the funeral service while Governor Cephas Msipa was addressing mourners. When they sang *Guide Me thou Great Redeemer*, the Lord God told me that the song was the one to be the anthem of the mission field where He was sending me. I wondered why a Welsh anthem was chosen for the mission field of America..

My faith grew stronger year after year. My salvation experience helped me from possible death from witchcraft over the years, as God fought for my life. Some people choose whether to be saved or not, but others have no other choice but to surrender their lives to Jesus Christ if they are to make it in this life. People's realities are very different. I knew from then on that my success in life had to be hinged on God.

In High School, at Nagle House, Marondera, I had another amazing fellowship with God. It was during my lower sixth and upper sixth years that God told me that He would call me to *"my people who are wounded"* I didn't quite understand what God was saying. Still, my call to America and my generation started then. As I began to prepare for university, I was clear that my field of study would be Law. During my preparation, God told me to change my plan. He told me to plan on studying Military Strategy. I had no idea what that was about, although I had read of a South African School of Strategy in a newspaper article, the program was not offered in Zimbabwe. It was not even listed as one of the areas of study by the University of Zimbabwe at that time. I only discovered the program when I diligently searched around campus during registration, that the program existed. I thanked my God and registered for the program. I had no idea that when God told me about the Military Strategy program, it had not been introduced at the University of Zimbabwe. It was only introduced at the beginning of the year that I started my studies. One of the lecturers told me how the program had been launched, and I realized that while

War and Strategic Studies was a great benefit to the military and the nation at large, it had a connection with my destiny in many ways. I liked the course content because I wanted to be a diplomat. I was the only female in the class from the second to the final year.

Chapter 6
Training to be an Intercessor

While studying at the University of Zimbabwe, the Holy Spirit trained me to intercede for my pastors and other people. I grew spiritually. God always warned me to avoid being in a group or following fads. He wanted me for Himself. I learned a lot as I prayed in the Swinton Hall bathroom when other girls had gone to sleep. The reason why God wants some lives to be set aside for Him alone is that some individuals may have a mandate to pioneer things in their lives. As such, the individuals may be sabotaged by friends or communities they belong to, to the extent of being diverted from total obedience to God. Family, friends, and authority figures are good sources of advice, but some of them cannot advise an individual in matters that they have never experienced. This is very common among pastors, and parents. They exert a lot of influence on individuals who are in their congregations, and family members. From experience, I realized that some of the things that God asked me to do were outlandish. Some pastors who were my shepherds wanted me to marry quickly soon after high school because they wanted me to be 'tamed.' They saw a wild girl who needed to be controlled. On the other hand, God warned me to be careful of blindly following people but to listen to God alone. It was all foreign because, during my early Christian years, pastors had a lot of influence on me. I realized that I antagonized some of them when I made decisions without consulting them. Even when I moved abroad, the Holy Spirit told me not to tell anyone what He was doing with my mission to America as He pointed out to me that *"Satan does not care whom he will use to block you. He will use trusted people as long as he can accomplish his plans"* Parents, on the other hand, are happier when they see their children act according to environmental guidelines. Children who are independent cause anxiety to the parents at times. I gave my parents many doses of that. They did not understand that when I spoke sometimes, I was prophesying within what appeared like a normal conversation. I did not understand it either. Many years later, I would hear family and friends say, "Do you remember that many years ago, you spoke about what is happening now?" Many members of my father's family asked me to tone down my bluntness. I would talk about the truth regarding how they live in a normal conversation, and many would be convicted about their lifestyle. Yet I knew nothing about the secrets of their lives. It was the Holy Spirit at work, convicting men of sin and judgment- John 16: 8. To remain connected to such a flow of the power of God, one has to live a consecrated life. I had many 'don'ts' from God because of what He was preparing me for in the future. I made many mistakes because I wanted to be a 'normal person, but God kept pressing me to walk the narrow and straight path. Even when I made a mistake, He would correct me and redirect me back to the life He wanted me to live. The calling of God does not happen overnight, it is molded in the normal day-to-day experiences.

I was aiming to join the Ministry of Foreign Affairs after graduation from university. Still, again, the Lord God redirected me to go and work for the Zimbabwe Broadcasting Corporation after graduation.

I had a specific mandate from God. My assignment was to pray for the airwaves to open up to the gospel. Before that, the broadcasting station had mainly Catholic and other mainline church services on radio stations, but God wanted the gospel to be preached on television as well. To accomplish that, God wanted an intercessor stationed at the station. When you have such a mandate, you face the darkness in the area of responsibility as you pierce it with light until it disperses. It is a battle. A very intense one too. I had a very hard time fitting in. I experienced untold harassment from some of my superiors. Once some senior management personnel knew that I was a Christian of the Pentecostal persuasion, they would not talk to me. When I met them in the hallways and corridors, they would look aside whenever I greeted them. Darkness, in any place, does not float around; it influences people's behavior and attitude. In fighting the darkness in any place, human beings are used as mediums of attack. Consequently, the intercessor will appear to be at loggerheads with other people. Yet, the spirits will be using people who are open and defenseless to achieve their plans in any place where they operate. The fight is often protracted. By this, I mean that darkness will not just disperse without putting up resistance. The airwaves were opened up, and godly programs were incorporated. At face value, the decision looked like a corporate decision, but prayer influenced policy. This is the power of prayer; it can change policies at the national or regional level if intercessors know how to work with God. God always wins. After some time, I discovered other believers at the station. Some had backslidden due to environmental pressure to desist from being churchy. Soon, the station had a church family that fellowshipped every lunch hour. Whether you like it or not, when God assigns you to such hard assignments, it is like being thrown to the deep end, where you choose whether to swim or drown. I learned the rules of engagement quickly, and the War Studies lectures came in handy during those times.

    I had no precedent for the mandate that God was giving me except for the ones in the Bible. So, I grew to like the exploits of personalities like Samuel the prophet, Elijah the Tishbite, Queen Esther, Ruth, Simeon, and Ana. I failed in some parts of my mandate because I wanted people to understand what was going on around me, and sadly they did not. When God takes over your life and your

parents reject you, He can make you eat from His hand, meet all your needs, and give you joy that you cannot understand. Psalm 27: 11 says,
Teach me Your way, O Lord. And lead me on a smooth path because of my enemies.
God adopts you and leads you into His perfect plan for your life. He treats you like a Father. I ceased to fulfill the agenda of man. When we have such a calling, God wants us to be relevant to our environment according to His plan. As a result, He starts to mold our characters in such a way that we go through situations in life that will empty us of whom we think we are until we can surrender completely. This is what you would call God's pedigree. Any other human pedigree carries the fallen human nature. When God has his hand upon a life, He also wants that person to marry a particular person for the ease of the flow of what He wants to do on earth. I have had failed relationships because the individuals concerned either came into my life before the right time, or were sometimes satanic agents seeking to destroy my life. I would also fail to perceive what God was saying to me about a potential suitor at times. All that helped me to realize that warfare surrounded the area of

relationships in my life. Jesus Christ learned obedience through the things that He suffered. *Hebrews 5: 8.* Imagine the very Son of God, walking on foot for miles, getting tired on earth that He created because He did not want to live in heaven without you and me. That is how I survived all forms of abuse because there were tender hands delicately holding me all the way. This is what God desires for all of His creation. God is such a Father to me to the extent that when he brought me to the man whom I was supposed to marry, He did not throw me at that young man. He said to me, *"Look carefully at this man. Is he not handsome?"* I responded to Father honestly, and He loves that, "This man is drop-dead gorgeous. I do not know what to do. I don't even know him that well, but O, boy! I had also pledged to myself that I would not date before I graduated from college" Father God would build up all the positive attributes of that man, and nothing seemed flawed. God could have given me the order to marry the young man, but He wanted everything to follow naturally. There are many examples that I can give about my interactions with my Heavenly Father, but I think that these examples are enough.

The second part of my mandate was to go and work in the countryside. God showed me a woman wearing a doek, working in the field. To God, the woman represented the Zimbabwean woman, and not the ones in urban areas. On that issue, the Lord God said, *"The women in the rural areas are not afforded equal time on the airwaves as their urban counterparts. They have no voice. I want you to go and work with women in the countryside and give them a voice because I raised you to be a voice of the voiceless"* God is an emancipator. He does it without militancy if those who are called to lead and to show compassion heed His voice to do right in the way that they handle their duties towards fellow human beings. That is how I ended up in Bindura as a news reporter. I had to go and work with country women.

I remember one of the board members of Zimbabwe Broadcasting Corporation. Claude Mararike, commenting on my news items on the bulletin. "Fortunate's reports are always on the less privileged. She has a passion for reporting on stories on the marginalized" Mararike amply defined part of my mission at the station without knowing that it was a divine mandate that I was executing. I spent eleven years on that assignment.

God was asking me to do more than be a voice of the voiceless in broadcasting but to dedicate my life to the restoration of other women. I was still going through the process of healing myself, but God was shaping the direction I should go concerning my calling. In the 90s, I assumed I would be that voice through broadcasting. That changed in 1998 when I was a guest speaker at a women's conference. I asked the Holy Spirit about the message for the conference. His response to me was, *"Go and talk about your rape experience."*

    The rape experience was not the good news of the gospel. It was my secret. A closely guarded one too. In amazement, I wondered whether God was speaking to me or another strange voice, but it was the Third part of the Trinity, the Holy Spirit. This was taboo to me! Thankfully, the Holy Spirit prepared me for the day. The Holy Spirit gave me an amazing sign. Days or a week before the convention, I felt like I had a little plastic bag nicely tucked just above my left breast, filled with a fluid that felt like water in a plastic bag. The Holy Spirit let me know that in that pouch was the message for the conference. For days, I carried the invisible pouch, and when I bent over, I would feel it move as well as if it was a plastic bag with water. That was the reminder that the word and anointing for the women's conference were ready to break like the alabaster ointment. It did not break before the convention, but on the day of the meeting, it dramatically. It was my first time talking about my closely guarded life secret of an episode of rape that I had had in the early 70s. Although I did not talk about it, I remembered every detail of what happened about three times in my bedroom. The rape did not happen in an impoverished environment but a fairly wealthy one, where I had a personal bedroom at five years old under the guardianship of well-to-do relatives.

As I spoke about my experience at the conference, I discovered that three-quarters of the women attending the conference were rape victims. That is when the pouch that was attached to the upper part of my left breast broke, and there was a sensation of rain falling into the atmosphere. I saw the desperation in the women as they struggled to muster enough courage to confront the violation that had been perpetrated against them. My heart was very broken at the site of the anguish suffered by the women. The cries were piercing, and the desperation horrendous!

Many emotions that had been bottled up for years among the older women, as well as the young, exploded in that environment. Bitterness! Anger! Confusion! Cries for mercy! Rolling on the ground! Eyes that looked at me, begging for an answer as to why such dastardly acts had been done to them. Others begged for embraces because the pain was unbearable, and they needed support to deal with it. The atmosphere was very tense, but an amazing thing was also happening as the invisible rain that I felt in the atmosphere was washing the women and girls. It was a cleansing encounter that left many women restored. I was only instrumental in the healing of the women, but the work was being done by the Holy Spirit. From that experience, I realized how deep the wounds of rape are and how hard it is to talk victims out of that kind of brokenness. I realized that only God, who made the woman knows the effect of rape on her well, and He is the only one who can restore or mend the brokenness. There are places in the human soul where psychology cannot go. It is a place reserved for the Spirit of God. When that has been tampered with, it is best to take the damaged goods back to the manufacturer because maintenance people can cause more damage.

After the conference, the Holy Spirit told me that this is the general condition of women in Zimbabwe, and God's heart is broken over their condition. He wants their deliverance from this violation and its consequences on their lives and relationships. I understood from then on that the emancipation of women in the countryside that God referred to had more to do with the violation of the core of their being. With that brokenness, economic progress and education would not be sufficient cures.

I realized that God sees the silent cry of the woman of Zimbabwe, and God cries, sitting by her side comforting her, but the woman yearns to hear Zimbabwe itself saying to the girl child, "Sorry for the pain that you have suffered unfairly for so long." However, God is also looking for someone to stand up and say, "What was done, has been done, and is being done to the woman or girl child in Zimbabwe is wrong" Granted, not all women are victims. Some are even perpetrators.

God had to take me through a process of deliverance before I could help others. In hindsight, I realize that my rape experience was a ritual. An act of worship at an altar that the adults around me knew of. After the violation at about five and a half, I regressed in behavior and started living like two-year-old needing napkins and potty training. I remember soling myself in my sleep. I would be taken out of the house and bathed in the middle of the night. There was no question asked, and there was no treatment sought. Life went on normally, but I was never the same. None of the adults who were my guardians did ask for once why I acted in the manner that I did. I even reached out to teach my little cousin what the boy from the village had taught me during the rape. I was disciplined for making such a move, but still, there was no desire to ask me where I had learned the behavior. I was kind to my cousin by teaching him what I had experienced. The rape was perpetrated by a boy from a local village. The village was far from our vicinity, but for some reason, the boy would come whenever the adults left on a shopping trip. Again, for a reason not known to me, I was always left behind on the shopping trips when the rape occurred, yet, I always traveled with the adults except for that brief season. The boy would come into my bedroom with freedom, and he would threaten me badly. I remember being shell-shocked and shivering with fear, and in that state, he would rape me. My cousin, who was at home, would never follow inside the house to check on me. It appeared like he was acting as security outside, ensuring that the young man had all the time that he wanted with me. I remember that there was a planned family vacation that I also was supposed to be a part of, but at the last minute, I was told that I could not go. I was left with the maid for about two weeks. I realized that I had to stay back because my purpose was to be at home all the time. After I was raped, even the maid sleeping in the kitchen, a part of the main house, was found having sex with the gardener.

    A year later, I started the first grade. It was a long walk to school. The gardener would help me to walk halfway, but after school, I walked home alone. A fifth grader befriended me. She invited me to pass through their house at the start of the second grade. Then she called me into her bedroom. The home was just as wealthy as the one that I lived in. The older girl threw me onto her bed as if she was playing with me. Then she told me that she wanted to show me something. It was like a relationship between a big sister and her younger sibling. Suddenly she jumped on top of me and started humping me as if we were having sex. We were dressed in our clothes, but she continued with the humping and only let me go after about five minutes. She had a lesbian spirit. But why did she find me an easy target? The spirit of rejection was bringing in its friends, rape, and perversion. This is designed to thwart any future chance of escape by the victim. This was an encounter with a lesbian spirit. Yes, a lesbian spirit in the village. When a cluster of demons attacks a person like that, the deliverance is difficult, Here is why? A sex addict can go into rehabilitation to deal with sexual addiction. However, at the end of rehabilitation, the person gains control of sexual urges but changes the gender preference for partners. This is because another spirit possessing the person has taken over control of the person. That also means that the person is not yet free. That change of preference is a manifestation of one of the domineering spirits in the person's life which may have been lying dormant until the right time. One telling sign that a person is not yet free is their denial of Jesus Christ's Lordship. Denial does not have to be violent, it can be expressed in very soft terms, but it is still a denial of the deity of Christ. Such a denial is ramped up by the satanic source of the spirits that possess the person. Very often, in western cultures, the person becomes curious about other religions and searches them out with diligence. Some people in developing nations get stuck to tradition religiously. They get stuck, and their ears are closed to any call for salvation. This is designed by demons to keep the person far from the saving power of the Cross of Jesus Christ. Salvation through Jesus Christ is a very expensive transaction. Yet, it appears very simple that people miss the opportunity for salvation because it is simple- *For the preaching of the cross is to them that perish foolishness; but unto us which are saved, it is the power of God (1 Corinthians 1:18)*

Only the blood of Jesus Christ can burn such clusters of demons out of their hiding places to the point of manifesting. When demons manifest, it is in their language, a way of asking to be told where to go when they leave the person under possession.

Some victims of sexual abuse become the wives of Satan through the same system of illicit sexual encounters. Such people are difficult to deliver unless the deliverer has attained a senior rank in the spirit, which comes with the grace to do so. I had no idea what the older girl was doing to me or what the action meant. Here is the issue; once the act of rape was perpetrated against me, a spirit was violently deposited into my life. To make sure that I was vile enough for Satan to have total control of me, the older girl was being used to introduce the spirit of lesbianism. I was a rejected child. That rejection from my father opened the door to a demonic attack. One can argue that we did not take off our clothes so how can the spirit of perversion be passed on. The truth is that the older girl was possessed, and she had been assigned to transfer the spirit to me. That did not require taking off clothes because it was a spiritual act. My father, whom God entrusted me with, believed I was not worthy of living, so Satan used that door to claim me as a rejected person for his personal use.

In the game of life, there is a big contention between darkness and light. Do not fool yourself that you can float around without God and think Satan will not bother you in that condition. You are already his, and he will get you to do his bidding whenever he wants you to. He sent a rapist my way, and a lesbian who completed the demonic oppression on my life as is written in Ecclesiastic 2:12, *And if one prevails against him, two shall withstand him. A threefold cord is not quickly broken.* The threefold cord of rejection, rape, and lesbianism were working together as a foundation to control my life for the future. I was delivered from satanic control when I got saved.

Many behaviors that we see in adolescents are a manifestation of seeds sown in their lives at birth or infancy. The seeds grow as the child grows, gradually shaping their taste and influencing the environments they encounter until their teenage years. Another thing to understand is that demons usually operate in a group of three. Even satanic agents that come to church services to attack the congregation come in groups of two or three. They mingle with the congregation with a plan to attack the whole church. Here is an example that can be given about the three-fold cord operation of demons. If a person has a witchcraft demon, that spirit will invite jealousy and lying. Usually, a person who steals lies, as well as engages in prostitution. If it is an accident, infirmity, disability, or death, it can form a threefold cord to kill a person. There was no way that I could have escaped that route in life, except that God intercepted the dangerous plan of destruction in my life when I got saved. If the born-again experience had been something that was not attractive to me in

1980, perhaps I could be a lost soul promoting all kinds of belief systems today. Many such people who were rejected, raped, sodomized, and molested ended up joining the LGBTQ community? This is food for thought for those among us who are always quick to condemn others, calling them vile without knowing their story. God, who has spoken to me since my salvation experience in 1980, pointed out that He had to make me go through such experiences so that I can be broken enough to understand the pain of others. As a result, God spoke to me also, saying that I did not need to go to Bible School or seminary because He would train me on what I should do in ministry. Who can be trained in a seminary about how to be broken? In my ministry in America, I have come across broken people in many ways, and my life experience has been such a source of strength and understanding of my clients and congregants.

There are a few things to glean from my rape experience. The environment in which something happens matters. Everyone who lived under the roof of our house was sexually active. From me to the adults, including the maid, and gardener, there was sexual activity. This is because there are environments dedicated to altars of one kind or another. In this case, the home was dedicated to sexual activity by the spirit that controlled the affairs of the environment. Therefore, every person who came under that roof would act under the legal requirements of the spirit in charge of the house. This is a spiritual law called the Law of Agreement. There are people you should never walk with because if you do, you may regret it because their assigned purpose could be to transport the spirit of death and they will pass it on you through association. It is even more dangerous if such a relationship is a marriage. Then whoever befriends them partakes of what they have because Amos 3:3 says *Can two walk together, except they are agreed?* The agreement law will affect you if you agree to walk with the person. The same applies to marriage.

Two people love each other and then enter into a covenant to seal their agreement to be lovers and to live together. Some couples become one so that they end up looking alike. I am explaining the fact that the environment that I was living under had ordinances that ruled it, and one of them was inordinate sex. The maid and gardener were fornicating. The older girl in the house was said to have innumerable boyfriends. It is more like mind

control. When you enter a place or associate with a person, you have no choice but to do what is defined by the ordinances of the place or your partner's life. If it is a house of God, David says, in Psalm 122:1, *"I was glad when they said unto me "Let us go into the house of the Lord"* An environment can define your attitude, shape your taste, and spur you into progress or failure, modulate your character, thereby giving you an identity. I became a victim of sexual abuse in the environment in which I lived. It was not just rape but an initiation into a life that was supposed to be distant from God.
Genesis 6 points out a phenomenon, *And it came to pass when men began to multiply on the face of the earth, and daughters were born unto them,*
2 That the sons of God saw the daughters of men that they were fair, and they took them wives of all they chose.
3 And the Lord said, My spirit shall not always strive with man, for that he also is flesh: yet his days shall be a hundred and twenty years.
4 There were giants in the earth in those days; and also after that, when the sons of God came in unto the daughters of men, and they bore children to them, the same became mighty men which were of old, men of renown.

5 And God saw that the wickedness of man was great in the earth and that every imagination of the thoughts of his heart was only evil continually.
6 And it repented the Lord that he had made man on the earth, and it grieved him at his heart.

The sons of God mentioned above were angels which had sex with women. They chose the women according to the last part of verse 2, which may imply the lack of consent from the daughters of men- girls. In Zimbabwe, some people worship a spirit with sexual relations with humans. That means that just like in Genesis 6, we are making God regret having created such a nation, which has given itself wholly to idolatry. This is the power of the environment on a person. The children born between the marriage of humans and spirits were called the Nephilim or giants. This is a group of people born outside the pattern of procreation ordained by God. Their DNA is not of God. They cannot be saved.

Is it possible that among us, due to the nature of our ruling deity, there could be much of the DNA that was not authorized by God? Yet, we say that we worship our ancestors through our system. However, the deity exercises its authority over the affairs of the land of Zimbabwe. Consequently, people under its jurisdiction are bound to behave in a certain way, and carry themselves in a way that conforms to the ordinances of the ruling spirit. The nation of Zimbabwe is ruled by a Nephilim spirit called Mulimo, which has its shrine at Njelele if the events in Genesis 6 are juxtaposed with what is happening in Zimbabwe.

At the hands of that deity, the church is struggling, and many are selling out to it because they cannot handle the warfare involved against it. Now is the time for a new generation to demolish this system and bring back the country to the worship of the One true God. We will see it in our time, and it will be sudden. Yes! Zimbabwe will be restored by God Himself because in Canaan, God Himself had to mastermind the land dispossession of the Canaanites because they had refused to repent.

I also invite you to take note of the age at which all those foundational influences were being made in my life. They were from conception, then five and a half to seven years. Then you will realize that life begins at conception, and Satan fights some people from the womb, and even when they make it to earth, he has his agents waiting to destroy them. Some among us may realize that Satan never despises a pregnancy or a baby because he knows that one day the pregnancy will produce a baby that may cause serious damage to his kingdom. I believe that my father had offered me to Satan as a pregnancy, but because my mother was a virgin, God honored her and spared my life. I know that some among us despise purity or chastity before marriage, but it can make the difference between life and death. My parents divorced, but I believe it was all for my protection because I had to be separated from my father to live. My father, was a fashion conscious man who had such a lover of living well and comfortably, but that was not the standard that God wanted me to peg my life on. Lack was my training ground. I never felt poor, although my environment screamed poverty. Although some members of my mother's family were very hostile, it was a matter of lesser evil, and by the grace of God, I still survived.

After my deliverance, I have done my portion of fighting back by the grace of God. I serve God with all my heart. Satan knows how to handle his enemies. He catches them young, and while we look at them as innocent clueless babies, Satan has a strategy for their demise, even at the formative stage. Can we also, as parents and guardians, have a positive attitude towards pregnancy, a newborn, and a toddler because their mission on earth does not unfold when they grow up, but they are born with it?

Chapter 7
Separation from my children

When I had my children, God told me to teach them all the basic things they needed to know before they reached the age of five without considering the age of their bodies. The reason that God gave me is that the spirit of a person has no age. A person's body is limited by time, needing to grow up and mature. The spirit in a man on the other hand can assimilate knowledge without any problem, even what we view as difficult material to comprehend. I did not know then that I would not see my children until after a decade. What I had taught them sustained them during our separation. When I moved to the United States, God instructed me to leave the children back in Zimbabwe. God instructed me to make sure I left them with passports for ease of planning their journey to join me soon after. It turned out to be a different story when I got to America. The level of adversity was beyond what I could deal with. I had never walked that kind of journey before. God Himself told me from Joshua 3:4 *"But keep a distance of about a thousand yards between yourselves and the ark. Don't go near it, so that you can see the way to go, for you haven't traveled this way before." – (Christian Standard Bible)* God made me know that He alone had control of the destiny of my children, and He was going to raise them in the way He wanted. He did, for ten years. I was anguished by that separation. I learned to live with it, until I accepted that I could not do anything about my separation from my children. I surrendered to God concerning that matter. God asked me to be like Hannah, the mother of prophet Samuel who chose to partner with God regarding her son, and the direction of the nation of Israel was changed. The separation was also needful for my protection from death. Here is how I can sum up the story of separation from my children because I have been called a scatterbrain for leaving my children in pursuit of fun. I shared with a friend what had happened before that decision was made.

In 1998, God showed me that my death was imminent. I saw myself in the clouds looking down on earth. My son was 17 months old at the time that I was supposed to die. I was shown the suffering that my children were going through after my death. My toddler was left alone in the sun with no food, and my daughter was suffering so much too. I was looking at them from the clouds, and I agonized, but I could not change the suffering of my children, I realized that I was no longer on earth.

Next, I was shown the mode of death. I would die in South Africa after stepping on a live electric cable and tripping soon after rainfall. At the time of the dream, I had never been to South Africa, and I wondered how that would happen. The time came in 1999 when I was cleared to go with the army to Operation Blue Crane in South Africa. My son was 17 months old.

Then from nowhere, in a desert, there was a storm. It all started while I was in the toilet. I stayed put until the rain was over. When I went outside, the death dream flashed before me as I looked at the cables that littered the ground.

I ran back into the bathroom and fell on my face in prayer. I pleaded with God because I knew that, at that time, the die was cast. I do not know how much time I spent in the bathroom, but when I rose to leave, there was no one in view. My companions had left for their tents. I had to look for security to accompany me to my tent late in the night.

Then God spoke to me. He said that I was not going to die a physical death. Instead, my marriage was going to die. After that prayer, one Zimbabwean soldier came to me and said, "You might as well enjoy life out here because you are going to be divorced when you go back." This was a strange statement. God was speaking through people around me, but I dismissed what they said because they were being opportunistic. My marriage fell apart on May 1, 1999, a day after my return from South Africa,

Then God went on to explain a principle. He told me that He had saved me from death and that death was still manifesting in my life through the divorce. God told me that He would send me on an assignment to do His work. Since he had delivered me from death. He would let me go on assignment without the children. This was a paradox to me. I believed that God had saved me from death so that I could be with my children, but He was telling me to go to a far country without them. His explanation to me that it was better to be separated from the children for a season than to be with them in an environment in which I would die and leave them forever. With understanding, I chose the option of being separated for a season than forever. That is how I left my babies behind. One was turning 5, and the other 9. As long as I had the assurance that I would see them again, I was willing to leave them. Especially when God assured me that He would take care of them. Every act of obedience sets you at variance with the world. God wants total obedience and not a fraction of it. Those moments may be characterized by shame. Yet the end of it all is life, which friends and family can never give us.

    Today, I look back, and I realize that had I followed tradition and said I would not leave my children, my life would have been cut short, leaving my children in turmoil.

When God asks us to do a hard task, always know that in it all is something good for you. I have survived a very dark season. I did not die in the time of trials.

I have been vilified by many for my decisions, but I have always known that my life is predicated on total obedience to God.

God had started preparing me for separation from my children earlier, but I was in denial because I am a hands-on mother. For instance, I paid school fees for my pastor's daughter as a gesture of kindness because I could afford it. When I was taking the check to the family, the Holy Spirit said, *"Make a covenant with me before you hand over the money. Due to this gesture of kindness that you have shown, your own children will never lack school fees whether you are there or not."* There came a season when what God said happened. The father of my children went on early retirement from his job, and I was in the mission field with no pay in terms of cash. Even in that season, the children remained in private schools until they left for America.

Not only that, when my children joined me, I was still working without a monthly income, but my children never lacked food, clothing, and shelter. Today, one is an Ivy League university student, and the other got a full scholarship to a prestigious law school. This is what happens to the pedigree of God. The pedigree of God rides in the high places of life. But there is a price that has to be paid through obedience in order to obtain blessings. We all want good names, and wealth. There is nothing wrong with that as long as we know that nothing good and lasting can come from a fallen human nature. We receive blessings when God wrestles with our human nature called 'self-will' until He prevails. That process is tough. As a result many people look for shortcuts in order to avoid the pain, even to the pint of quitting. I could have done anything in my power to avoid separation from my children, but the divine mandate on my life required that I separate not only from my children, but also romantic connections. Those were tough choices but I made them, and survived. Not because of my own strength but through divine help. The two incidents traumatized me to the point of wiping out some memory slates on my conscious mind. I gradually regained my memory but some facts were erratic until after about a decade. I met former college students who were very close to me during college but I could not remember them until after a while. It is no mean chore to go through the process of dying to self, and live only on the will of God. I was a strong willed person who did not take no for an answer as well as being a possibility thinker. I could always find my way through things because that is how I had survived as a child. So, being told to dump someone you love for no reason threw my little mind into a frenzy. It got even worse when I had to turn away my back on my children as if I did not know the value of motherhood. I died many times but I now live to Christ. This is the simplest way to put it.

Chapter 8
Romance, and Destiny

In 1990, I bumped into a young man whom I had had a crush on for many years during my college years on Rezende Street in Harare. It is even hard to call it a crush because I did not make a conscious decision to get his attention. I had an uneasiness around him that made me very uncomfortable. I had never been in love although I was a survivor of rape. To be honest, I did not know what love was. I was a very free spirited person, but my heart was totally closed out to men. However that young man had an effect on me that is hard to describe. I was not looking for love, but his eyes seemed to beam with a message that made me wonder. This man was my first love. By the time that I met him after college, we had known each other for four years.

I had come from the broadcasting station and wanted to do some shopping, then I saw him, and was excited to see him, just as he was seeing me. We started dating soon after. I had been struggling to find a date in my church, more so because God had told me that I had no future in that church. I loved the church, but I knew that if my future was not there, it meant that even my partner was not in that church. I tried to date in the church, but nothing seemed to work out. I prayed for the right partner, and the one with whom I felt very attached showed up after a year.

That young man understood my boldness and strength of character, which covered up a lot of brokenness, but was nevertheless needed for survival. He handled that package of my personality very well. For the first time, I could look up to a man with trust. Whatever he said seemed to be right all the time. I saw no reason to argue or resist what he said because he seemed to have all the right answers. I admired and respected him. That was very rare for me. I had had other suitors, but the Lord would always disqualify them, but the Lord did not say anything negative about that young man; instead, God rooted for him. I would audibly hear a voice directing me to this man saying *"Look at how handsome he is. Is there anything that you can say is wrong with his looks?"* For some reason, I thought that the young man was also hearing what I was hearing, and that made me shy around him. Things got heated up, and we wanted to do everything right, and the relationship was pure as we waited to go to the altar, where my father would hand me over to my future husband.

    From nowhere, the Lord told me to terminate the relationship with immediate effect. The young man was my little world. I was very confused, and that is even an understatement because the breakup was so devastating to me that I lost the drive that I had for life, and I sank into a depression. In obedience to God, I picked up the phone and called him to break up what I had hoped would be a lifetime relationship with my first love. I was crying in the process. Only one friend of mine called Tsitsi joined me one weekend, and as we lay on the bed with our legs stretched on the wall, she, in typical fashion said "Fortue, what happened? You seem to have lost that drive which is typical of you" I did not answer her at all because I did not know what to say. Could I blame God or myself? A faithful friend will always tell you the truth.

God is very gracious. He told me I needed to break up the relationship because we could not be together then. After all, I would face a lot of adversity in my future, and the Lord did not want my boyfriend to be involved in what I would face. God made it clear that the road ahead was going to be very rough, that there was no guarantee that I would live through it, and that my boyfriend was not supposed to go through that phase. God gave me very plausible reasons, but that did not stitch back my heart. The Lord told me, *"True love can let go. If you love him, then let him go"* I had no plan B. My ex-boyfriend was very protective of me. There was nothing to fear in his company. He understood me in a way that no one else could match. I could not say the same of the ensuing years without him when I tried to date again. I was broken trying to find my ex-boyfriend among other men, but it was a mess.

I eventually married another man in rebellion against God because I thought God did not care for me. After all, He was always saying "*No*" to my choices. I was on the run, trying to hide somewhere so that I could live. So, I thought! People around me saw a very happy, confident person, but something had invaded my life that had turned it upside down, gnawing at my life. My life became a nightmare. I had no support system. I had to come up with one quickly, and in that confusion of perspective, I decided to get married. I felt a net closing in on me, and I did not have any way out. After my marriage, God told me that because He did not sanction my marriage, it had to be weighed in His scales to determine whether it should continue, and if it failed, then that would be the end. It was a strange marriage. I was duped into visiting the family, but they were not welcoming. When we got married, a sister-in-law came to me and said, "I left my husband because I want your husband to take care of me." It was the strangest statement from an in-law, but I soon realized there were stranger things. Eventually, the marriage failed the test and ended like a vapor. In that marriage, I encountered bizarre experiences. To this day, I thank God because I do not know how I did not lose my mind. The sexual attacks in the dreams continued from many angles. I remember, one night, I woke up to an experience where something was licking my left-hand fingers. It had sharp teeth, and its saliva was drooling down my fingers. I did not withdraw my hand, but I just passed out.

When I woke up the following morning, I collapsed in the bathroom and was taken to the hospital. They suspected an ectopic pregnancy, but it was not. I sent a message to my father telling him about my illness. My father responded by saying 'She ain't seen anything yet," Meaning that more weird experiences were yet to come my way from my father. I went back to the hospital often due to strange illnesses, and the doctor finally told me, "If you continue like this, you will die on the operating table." I was dying for sure. It was a matter of time.

Then members of my church who were prayerful began to teach me how to do warfare against anti-marriage spirits. The church had an anointing for deliverance. One thing that they taught me was the importance of fasting for twenty-four hours so that I could break covenants made against me at night too. Bizarre things happened in the house. I would hear a person say a curse word in the house, and when I looked around, there was nobody except me. I would fill two trolleys (carts) of groceries for a family of three plus a maid, and it would vanish in less than two weeks. This was a lot of food, but it appeared we were feeding a crowd. As we prayed, change came, and I began to win, but my relationship with my father ended. I confronted him about his efforts to sacrifice me for the sake of his business. He had never been challenged like that before. I realized that there are things that you have to challenge to weaken them. My father formally disowned me for telling him to stop a practice that he knew of very well and was deeply engaged in. He believed in what he was doing as much as I believed in the power of God to deliver me.

    I would have motor vehicle accidents, which my father acknowledged that he had caused. The reason was that I had challenged him to stop his ritual acts of sacrificing me. My father was ready for the fight. He vowed to put my mother in a wheelchair because he claimed that she was the one influencing me wrongly, and then he would take me out of the land of the living, but God is stronger. My father failed in both instances. My mother, Neldah, had to get saved and learn to pray warfare prayers for her to survive. It was an interesting dynamic in which a staunch Lutheran experienced a salvation encounter with Jesus Christ, and got spirit filled. She recounted an incident in which the Holy Spirit told her that a man was sent to attack her. The man was on his way according to the Lord. However, my mother was told that "The man who is coming is not human. He is from the graves. But I have nullified his mission against you" For sure, after a few days, my mother woke up to the voice of a man talking to her from outside her bedroom as he stood by the window. The man said, "Neldah, I have been sent for you. I am taking you with me" My mother, began to fast and pray. She told me that she had fasted for three days during that incident. She never told anybody. After three days, the man showed up again at the window and said, "You are burning me up, I am going back"

The Lord instructed me to separate myself from my father, but the attacks continued. The family that I had married into had its challenges relating to a practice that related to sexual immorality.

One incident was devastating, but many other experiences were equally bad. After a funeral at his family home, my ex-husband brought back a pair of boxer shorts that he received while distributing the clothing of a dead brother. I wanted to throw away the tattered boxer shorts, but then I felt that I was being insensitive to another person's grief. I decided against my better judgment to leave the cloth in the bedroom. That night, I had a dream, let me call it, an open vision of another brother who was still alive coming onto the bed wanting to have sexual relations with me. I jumped up from the bed as I called out his name. I shouted out the name and then sat down in shock. My ex-husband was fast asleep as I was going through the whole ordeal. I looked at the boxer shorts and realized that it was carrying some spiritual force that we gave access to our house by keeping them. This is not superstition; it is the reality in some families. Someone had placed some spirit on the torn shorts. After pointing out what my brother-in-law had attempted to do to me, the family took a stance that I did not belong in their family anymore and that I should be divorced.

    I realized God had been my father, protecting me from my earthly father. It is hard to talk like this, but I must be transparent because some people in worse off situations will read this book and be emboldened to stand up to abuse. Many boys and girls are so condemned by tradition to the point of dying at the hands of their family because they were told that they cannot challenge their parents even when they are unfairly treated. God asked in Colossians 3:21, *Fathers, do not embitter your children, or they will become discouraged.* My father fought me like an enemy because I refused to bow down to his idolatrous ways or submit to being sacrificed in a business ritual. God helped me to separate myself and be out of range of constant attacks from him. My stepmother wrote my ex-husband a letter asking him to divorce me. The letter was sent to the workplace so that he alone would see it. He brought it to me and said, "This is a letter from your mother."

At one time, I missed my father so much, and when I had a business trip that passed through his town, I sent one hundred United States dollars to him. I did not know how to relate to him anymore. I had obeyed him as a child, which was not good enough. I wanted him to walk me down the aisle on my wedding day, but he did not want me to get married. I brought my first child to meet him, and he cursed her out. When I gave his neighbor the money to take to him, I was worried about what the outcome would be. By the end of that evening, I was admitted to the hospital for three days with machines connected to my body. The hospital staff wondered what was wrong with me, but I was very sick. I knew in my heart of hearts that the money had reconnected me to the evil flow of darkness again. What do you do as a child who only wants to make parents happy but no matter what you do the parents are not satisfied? I bought my father a suit, and then he said "Where are the shoes?"

I regretted ever sending the money because I knew I was courting trouble. There are spiritual dynamics that would take too long to elaborate on at this point. I decided to stay away from my father until he died. Just before his death however, the Holy Spirit instructed me to write him a letter and apologize for what had happened between us. I wrote the letter, and it got to him just before he died. It is hard to fall from being a daddy's girl to an archenemy. The pain of knowing that this was not the first time that my father had rejected me was horrendous.

I only heard that before my father died, he expressed regret that "My obedient child who never disrespected me for once is so distant from me." He cried many tears of regret. That did not worry me because he was only regretting it. After all, God had protected me from him; otherwise, he could have killed me as part of a sacrifice. I was very close to him and forgiving of how he had abandoned me in my childhood, but he never seemed to change from his plan of using me for his own gain in an occult ritual. This is a rampant belief system in Zimbabwe, and it tears families apart, and unless measures are taken to address the effects of witchcraft, the occult, and child sex abuse, the nation remains in grave sin. I am not pointing this out because I was victimized by the system; I am grateful that I escaped many snares and very few women and men have succeeded in doing so. My stepmother visited me in my dreams and once said, "I am sorry for what I did to you." In response, I said to her You know how much I loved you. Why did you decide to be so cruel to me? The dream ended, and I knew God wanted me to forgive her and move on. I tried.

Chapter 9
Careers:

From Journalist to Iron and Steel Industry Public Relations, and then to the mission field of America

In the struggle to go our separate ways as the relationship was dying, the Lord told me that I should join the Zimbabwe Iron and Steel Company- ZISCO.

Here is how I Joined the Zimbabwe Iron and Steel company- ZISCO. The Holy Spirit told me, "You need to run for the presidency of The Zimbabwe Union of Journalists- ZUJ." I submitted my candidature. The meeting was held at the Golden Mile hotel in Kwekwe. That morning, the Director General of ZISCO was sitting at the hotel, reading a newspaper. It was kind of early, but he was there. I greeted him, and I told him that I was running for the presidency. He wished me luck, and then he left immediately. I had no idea that he was scouting for a Public Relations Manager. He was looking at the candidates to see who among them was bold enough to run for the presidency. That person would have the boldness to handle ZISCO. I marketed myself to him by running for the presidency, and I got the job. I did not win the ZUJ presidency because that was only a means that the Holy Spirit used to get me into the new job.

The new job had a mandate from God too. God told me that *"I have compassion for the people who live in Torwood. If the steel company closes down, these people have nowhere to go. Therefore, I want you to go into the company and pray that it does not close down so the people will be sustained."* It was a three three-year stint that I did very well professionally in, but my personal life was a mess. The divorce had thrown me back into a world of dating that I was the most inexperienced in and which I also hated. Since the breakup with my first love, I could never give my heart wholly to any other person because that would be hypocrisy of the worst order. Nevertheless, I tried to be human but did not do very well. I tried to date, and it was all wrong.

At that point, I didn't care much about life because I was being hunted down by private investigators hired by my ex-husband. The private investigators called me up and told me the whole story. I did not expect the level of cruelty that my ex-husband showed to me and the children. Before the investigators called me up, the Holy Spirit called me to fast and pray for 21 days. I obeyed. In the process, one of the investigators wanted to play us against each other and decided to call me up, hoping that I would hire him, also. I did not give in to the suggestion, but I realized I was always trailed by unknown people.

I tried dating an ex-suitor without the intention of being serious at all because we were friends, but it was a wrong move. Thankfully, my pastors realized I needed support and helped me out of that relationship. The Lord was merciful to me. He then explained to me that *"Your destiny is connected to your marriage. As a result, it is the area of your life that you are experiencing the worst adversity. From now on, do not date any man until I tell you to do so.*

Otherwise, you will be killed if you try to make your own choices." From that conversation, I understood that even the rape in childhood was a preemptive strike on my marriage because it robbed me of a natural gift that I would have brought to my husband on our wedding day, my virginity. To this day, I do not know what it means to be a virgin. It was taken away very early on in life to the extent that it is as good as having not existed in my life.

The Andrae Crouch connection

In August 2001, Andrae Crouch, the American gospel music legend, came to Zimbabwe on tour. The Lord had told me that Andrae was coming before the announcement of his tour was made, but I still needed to learn how that tour was connected to me. Andrae Crouch came through our church for two concerts in Gweru and Harare, and I was assigned to guide the team during the tour. When I met Andrae and his group, I forgot the vision that the Lord had given me of him until he had left the country. In the vision I saw before he came to Zimbabwe, Andrae came to me, and he was very shy. That was his personality in real life. He came alive in his performances of music on stage. The place where he met with me in that vision was at his church in Pacoima, in the San Fernando Valley of California. I did not know the place's name in the vision, but I walked on his church grounds while still in Zimbabwe. I did not know who he was either, except that he was very kind to me, and the Holy Spirit trying to bail out my ignorance, said the initials of this man are A.C. I have always found the Holy Spirit to be very romantic in the manner in which he handles matters of the heart between people. In other words, I was taken in the spirit of America to be introduced to Andrae Crouch, as well as to tour his church. A church that I would one day service for eleven years, yet in that vision, I was clueless about what was going on save the joy I experienced from the kindness of the shy man.

    In the vision, Andrae was eager to show me the world. He did not utter a word but communicated in body language; he beckoned me to go up a hill. We moved from the church grounds and climbed a hill in that vision. When we got to the top of the hill, he stretched his hand to show me a panoramic view of distant lands as we stood on top of a hill that had broadcasting satellite dishes that faced four

different directions. I exclaimed, "This is panoramic." He responded with a smile and then guided me down the hill with gentleness back to the place which I later recognized as Christ Memorial Church, where he pastored a church that was founded by his parents under the Church of God In Christ. Then the vision ended. I completely forgot about the vision during his tour of Zimbabwe.
During his tour of Gweru and Harare, Andrae Crouch was very flirty with me. in his interaction to the point of asking if I wanted to go to the United States. I dismissed that as a typical celebrity lifestyle. I also had no clear incentive to do so.

    My life at face value looked great, but I was on the run from unseen forces. I had very real spiritual battles in my life. I was refusing to obey the instruction that I was receiving from God that I should sign the divorce papers and hand over all the properties to my ex-husband. It was like God was telling me that what I had worked for and built up was an abomination to Him. Therefore, there was nothing from that marriage that I was supposed to take with me except for the children, and a token settlement fee, to enable the paperwork to go through the divorce court. Andrae Crouch toured

Zimbabwe at a time when I was working on settling the divorce. Andrae made it clear that he knew what was going on in my life. Looking back, I realize that his offer was a lifeline and not just a romantic gesture when I think of it now. The politics at ZISCO, a partly government-owned company, eventually caught up with me without mercy, but my bosses were very supportive. ZISCO was a political melting pot, with different government factions jostling over what should be the way forward for the company. Only then did I develop a desire to leave the company.

Something worth mentioning is the heavy spiritual warfare that confronted Andrae Crouch in Zimbabwe, to the point of people dying. About three days before Andrae's arrival, there was labor unrest at ZISCO, which resulted in the deaths of two workers. While it was an internal problem, the death of two innocent people got me locked down in Redcliff to respond to the media. Not only that, the national Joint Operations Command- JOC also came to Zisco on the evening that I was supposed to receive Andrae at the airport in Harare. I almost gave up hope of ever participating in the tour because things were messy at my job. By the grace of God, I managed to leave Kwekwe very late and got to the airport just in time to receive the guests. The group proceeded to Kwekwe the following day to rest and prepare for a gig in Gweru. That night Andrae Crouch's arm was cut with a sharp instrument while he slept. The following morning, he had a deep dry wound that was not bleeding, but the white part of his flesh could be seen due to the depth of the incision.

At the concert in Gweru, Andrae met a nine-year-old boy, Jeremiah Mutsakani, who was a fledgling piano player. At the sight of Jeremiah, Andrae began to weep. Jeremiah was only nine years old, but Andrae said that he had seen the little boy about thirty years before that meeting on that day, and Jeremiah had said to Andrae, "Come over to Africa and help us" Andrae Crouch was overwhelmed by the fulfillment of that vision, and he cried for a while. That night, a new season for Andrae was born as he stood face to face with the connection to his new assignment to Zimbabwe. That connection was in the form of a nine-year-old Jeremiah. I did not realize that when Andrae appeared like he was flirting with me, he was very serious, as I came to know later on. He was a very shy man, just as I had seen him in the vision before he visited

Zimbabwe, and for him to come out to a stranger to express his desire for a relationship was a very bold move for a man of his character.

I believe God had a plan to develop the gospel music industry of Zimbabwe to cushion the nation from the economic turmoil that would come after, especially from 2008 onwards. Andrae said to me, "The talent is there in Zimbabwe, and we just need to focus on building their capacity" I saw Andrae devote time to mentoring younger musicians over the years at his church in Pacoima. Talent and character are important in public life. In the new millennium, executing a capacity-building project for upcoming musicians was a no-brainer because the broadcasting policy of Zimbabwe had created a conducive atmosphere by requiring 75% of broadcast content to be local. Music produced in that area could reach the audience sooner than before. This is the mandate under which Andrae Crouch came to Zimbabwe.

During his tour of Zimbabwe, Andrae had two concerts in Harare and Gweru. In Harare, the Ministry of Foreign Affairs hosted a dinner in honor of Andrae Crouch and his team. From

Zimbabwe, Andrae Crouch proceeded to Kenya.

Chapter 10
The death of my brother

Exactly a year after Andrae's tour of Zimbabwe, my only brother, born to my mother Tonderai, from another relationship, died suddenly. The report got to me that he had committed suicide.

I drove to Beitbridge, where he was supposed to have committed suicide, and found the whole community with many questions about his manner of death. The local people said that the young man did not exhibit any signs of a person who committed suicide. I did not know whom to believe. I was grieving, but I had to be strong for my mother. I asked my cousin, who had come to support us at the funeral, to help me get a postmortem. He responded, "Why bother yourself over someone who killed himself?" I ended the conversation immediately because I realized that while the local community where my brother lived strongly believed that my brother had been killed, my mother's family seemed to shoot down that narrative. People in the community went on to say that they heard the young man crying for help before he 'was killed. I prevailed with my plan for a postmortem. It was a public holiday. I wanted to have the young man buried in the town where he had died, but my aunt, who lived in the community, adamantly opposed the idea, choosing to transport the body to the countryside. She did not pay a dime for the funeral costs but made all the decisions without consulting my mother. The body was taken to Bulawayo for the postmortem, after which it was ferried to the village for burial.

    I was planning on joining the family in the village for the burial, but God, who has preserved my life from birth, showed up in His mercy. The Holy Spirit had an audible persuasive conversation with me. "*You see your brother who has died. He was not the target. You were. I allowed it, but the arrow of death was meant for you. Now they are waiting for you in the village. They want you. If you go to this funeral, you will not come back because you will be dead. They are waiting to physically kill you. I have plans for you to go to America, but if you attend this funeral, that plan will not come to pass because you will be dead. Do not go to that funeral."*

I sobered up. I realized that members of my family were eager to peddle the suicide story. Privately, I told my mother that I was sorry that I would not be able to attend the funeral. I did not give her the reason then. I prepared for all that would be needed for the funeral and then drove back to ZISCO. None of my relatives knew that I was not attending the funeral. I am told that they went into a frenzy when they realized that I did not show up. My mother's family then changed the narrative and said my mother and I had killed the young man. They also wondered how I had known about the plans that they had to hurt me. One of my aunts said, "She needs to thank whoever told her not to come because if she had showed up, my brothers were going to teach her a lesson." From this, and many other remarks, my mother realized that some family members were unhappy that they had not killed the right person. Instead of grieving with her, they ganged up to fight her throughout the funeral, upset that I had not shown up. We then realized that my brother's death was not a suicide but a possible planned murder. We had no proof of that.

Moreover, the anger exhibited by particular members of our family made us realize that there was more to the death of my brother than what we knew. I was finalizing my divorce after deciding to obey God and settle for what God wanted me to take at the end of the marriage. My father had declared war on me because I had fought off his plans to use my life as a ritual sacrifice. Then through the enlightenment of the Holy Spirit, I discovered that my mother's family had plans to murder me at my brother's funeral too. Under such circumstances, you know that it is a matter of time before the net closes on you. I think of many women and girls who died because they were trapped by their families, without room for escape. I had God on my side. The God who specializes in breaking snares of death broke the one set for me in Zimbabwe in 2002- Psalm 124:7 *Our soul has escaped as a bird from the snare of the fowlers; The snare is broken, and we have escaped.*

My life was under siege. The only people on my side were my mother and my two children. One of my sisters joined my mother's family in standing up against me. My children were too young to understand what was going on. Had the door to come to the United States not opened up, I would have died less than a year of my brother's death. Unfortunately, my other sister died also under bizarre circumstances while I was already in America. None of my mother's family came to her funeral. My mother buried her alone, with her son-in-law and the local community. None of her relatives who live in Zimbabwe paid their condolences until about six years later. For the first time in 2002, I realized that family could turn on you without mercy. I did not know why and when that attitude against me from my mother's family had developed to the point of wanting to wipe me and some of my siblings out. The Holy Spirit warned me to avoid gatherings because I was no longer safe. I was hiding from my family while I waited to leave the country. As a person, you reach a point where you ask yourself this genuine question "Did I ever belong to these people who I call family? If so, how can people come together to plot the demise of one of them without mercy? I believed in them even though the signs of animosity punctuated most of our relationships. I do not remember a day that I had turned my back on any of my family members, whether they were in-laws, my father's, and my mother's families, but here they were being exposed by heaven that their intentions on me were wicked. It is important to know that a satanic plan to destroy a person is easier to carry out if their family members harbor envy and jealousy, which rages within the people until they commit murder. When that is accomplished, the murderers can even regret and live with the guilt. That mental state can cause them to live miserably or even die. No one wins in hate-filled relationships. When a person exhibits jealousy, you can be sure that a spirit of murder is very close by and can express itself through that person using jealousy. Yet, society does not educate individuals on the dangers of envy or jealousy.

After the funeral of my brother, my mother's siblings changed the narrative of the death of my brother. They began viciously attacking my mother and accusing us of killing my brother through witchcraft. They were so eager to maintain that narrative that when it was confirmed that the young man had been murdered and his murderers were arrested and tried, none of our family members told me and my mother. They acted as the deceased's parents in the prosecution of the killers from beginning to end. They never told my mother about the murder case. I only got to know that the people who had killed my brother in 2002 had been prosecuted as late as 2021, almost twenty years down the line. It was my mother's cousin who told me, but members of my family have remained quiet about it while still pushing their narrative unashamedly. All the people involved did not know that I had been made aware by God to escape imminent death from them. I talk about this in celebration of God's mercy, but I also wonder where I would be if God had not tipped me about my family's plans and what narrative they would have given to the world. How many people have died at the hands of family, and the real cause of their death was never known because powerful relatives destroyed the evidence, or worse still, the victims were turned into the accused.

 As a pastor who comes from such a background, I have been taught by the Lord Jesus Christ through His Spirit not to accept what people say at face value, especially in church. I realized that once a family starts accusing a person, even outsiders join in, spreading the same lies. When a person finds out that they are rejected everywhere they go, they sometimes engage in self-destructive behavior, and if they die, they are still condemned and judged unfairly. Only God is the best judge in such matters.

Witchcraft operates with accusation, the pronouncement of judgment, and a verdict is passed on the accused. That is why some people will push for an argument with another person for no reason. While the argument appears like an unprovoked encounter with the witch, it will be the witch's way of trying to open the door of attack on the targeted person through anger, verbal response, or counteraccusations. When witches establish an open door through accusation, they can try the person and sentence them. The verdict could be death through an accident, poisoning, murder, drowning, or any other mishap. The Bible says in Proverbs 18: 21 *Death and life are in the power of the tongue, and those who love it will eat its fruits.*

The force of witchcraft

When James Salter, who was the son-in-law of Smith Wigglesworth, points out that during his missionary tour of the Congo, people engaged in eating other humans as late as the 1900s (Sumrall, 1995). One wonders if the advent of Christianity failed to destroy the practice of humans eating another human but shifted the practice from daytime to nighttime. With the abundance of wildlife in Africa in general, why would anyone choose to eat the flesh of another human being unless there is a mystery behind the practice? The Bible talks of the mystery of iniquity in 2 Thessalonians 2:7. Is it possible that humans find themselves helplessly shackled by this mystery which was initiated by the fall of Adam and Eve in the Garden of Eden? Under such circumstances, people find pleasure in vile ways because that is what is handed down to them by their ancestors.

    Yet, iniquity is an inherited sin, and such people cannot please God. Iniquity increases its strength and vileness from generation to generation. That is why Jesus said that *"And because iniquity shall abound, the love of many shall grow cold"*- Matthew 24:12. This mystery of iniquity, which is an expression of the fallen nature, causes humans to diminish the value of each other to the point of wanting to kill or murder. My challenge has been how to love people sold out to the force of iniquity until they turn from vileness to the fear of God. I realized that all the expressions of iniquity are powered by force introduced in the Garden of

Eden, and humanity is helpless before it without a Savior. That is why Jesus Christ came into the world.

My encounter with Lucifer

Through it all, I began to question who was coordinating the endless accusations against my mother and me. The force seemed to have a capacity larger than human beings. In my case, the people I called family seemed to have condemned me to death. I did not question and wonder about that for too long to get the answer in 2002.

Satan himself came to confront me one night. Then I realized that all the families fighting me were recruited into a high-level spiritual battle against my life to take me out before I could leave for America to fulfill a missionary mandate. I now believe that none of my family knew why they hated me so much because some of them would feel guilty and apologize later. Satan was the mastermind, but he used people whose lives were open to him through hatred, envy, and jealousy When Satan realized that he could not stop God's plan for my life, using the closest people to me, he showed up in person. Can you imagine the level of despondency when you live a life of rejection from birth, and the people who reject you, accuse you always so that you never have a chance to say a word to prove your innocence?

When you know that the battle is at a higher level and your family is being used because the members made a choice to submit to Satan instead of serving God, then you can learn to forgive. Still, you also develop the wisdom to stay away from such toxicity. Many women cannot escape, while some, even if they escape, are ignorant of the dynamics around their lives, so they venture back into the same environment that can spell doom over their lives. My crime against my family, as I gathered later, was that my prayers were hindering their plans, but the plan to fight me had started in childhood, if not at conception. The enmity was echoed in all three families. Yet most of those people go to church on Sunday. Whom are they worshiping?
Some of my family members passed on the hatred of me to their children. They told them

more lies and then concluded that when they die, their children should pick up where they left off in their fight with me. My crime is that I am a believer in Jesus Christ, and that aggravates them.

After August 2002, I started hearing a call from a distant land to go to C-Memorial-C. I still needed to learn what the place was and where it was. However, the distant call continued for weeks on end. Then one night, a man showed up in my bedroom around three o'clock in the morning. I opened my eyes to see a man walking around at the foot of my bed. When he realized that I was awake, he had one question for me, *"Are you sure that you want to marry Andrae Crouch?"* In my previous book, *The New Millennium Missionary: Passionately Pursuing the Call of God (2018, Revised),* I did not include this statement, but it was the opening statement that Lucifer said in my encounter with him. In that book, I had sifted through the information and decided to talk about the calling and not the romantic part. I was amazed by the question, but the man was serious and required an answer. Startled, I was not sure of what to say. Then suddenly, on my right, a wind welled up around me in a stationary position, but in a motion that is hard to explain. I knew somehow that it was the Holy Spirit. Without delay, the stationary billowing motion told me to respond to the man at the foot of my bed, saying, "*Say yes*" I did as I was told, and the man asked the question again. The Holy Spirit told me to respond with a "*Yes*" again, which I did. Immediately, the man turned to someone unseen, saying, "*You know that Andrae Crouch deserves to die. Why are you stopping me from killing him? You know he is a spent force, but you are still keeping him alive. You are even sending him a wife to help him. You know that he deserves to die. You know that he does not deserve this woman whom you are sending to him*" *Lucifer turned to look at me and said,* "*Look for a younger pastor; Andrae is too old*" The unseen person being addressed by Lucifer did not respond at all.

    After Lucifer finished his argument, it reminded me of the first two chapters of the Book of Job in the Bible, where Satan petitioned for the life of Job. I realized that the man at the foot of my bed was none other than Satan/ Lucifer himself. I wondered why it was so important for him to confront me in those early hours of the morning. From what transpired in my bedroom, I realized that I had been allowed to sit in the court of heaven where the life of the gospel singer Andrae` Crouch was contested by Satan. He was petitioning God to allow him to kill Andrae Crouch. After Satan's closing arguments on the case, the Holy Spirit told me to respond to him, just like in a court of law, which I did. I declared that "If Andrae is old and a spent force, then I am willing to go and help him as his wife" After which Satan looked at me in a way that I can only describe as threatening because it was still night, but then the issue was happening in the spirit, allowing me to understand some dimensions of speech even in the dark, and then he disappeared. I was alone in my bedroom again, but you cannot shake the feeling that the scene could still be playing out in the same room, except that your vision is not allowed access into that dimension.

Chapter 11
My mandate in California

Soon after my encounter with Lucifer, the Lord came to me and said, *"I need you stationed in California. It is very urgent. You will leave the children behind because the mission is hard. I am sending you to Andrae Crouch as a gift to him and his church. Because you are a gift to my servant, you will arrive there on Christmas day. Satan has the plan to kill Andrae Crouch before his time. Andrae is my servant who has been faithful to Me. He cannot die now because he has not yet finished his connecting generation assignment. You will pray for him, so he does not die before his time."* With that and other changing circumstances, I left for California. A ZISCO customer paid for my way to California. I kept wondering why Lucifer had said that Andrae deserved to die and that he did not deserve the wife God was sending to him. Andrae Crouch was not an ordinary person. He was a living legend of gospel music. I was a former news reporter and a public relations practitioner. There was no basis for any comparison. Why had Lucifer chosen to challenge God in that relationship? I immediately remembered that Lucifer is a father of lies. Either he was trying to sow seeds of pride in me or presenting a legitimate argument before God over a known case between him and God. I have never understood the gist of what happened in that room that night, except that my relationship with Andrae received one of the stiffest oppositions that I have ever encountered when I joined him in California. It took eleven years of battle for Andrae to live from 2001 until 2015. By the time that he died, I had already been released from the assignment and moved on.

From Andrae's encounter with Jeremiah Mutsakani, I understood what God meant when He talked of Andrae having the assignment to connect generations. Not only for those in Zimbabwe but the world over. Andrae was very excited about the new season of his life. He said to me in one of our discussions, "I want to bring the boy Jeremiah out here, as well as Admire." Admire was another young man from Zimbabwe. None of those plans came through.

There was so much bitterness among some pastors and believers back in Zimbabwe who failed to discern what God was doing at that time, as they questioned why I had jumped up and followed Andrae Crouch. They were just some of the ones who were short-sighted. Even people around Andrae saw me as an impostor who had no direction. For the first time, I realized the downfall of some black people in many instances. It is the lack of vision. Everything has to be about them before they think of a broader picture of things. I was very saddened when I saw the lack of vision through vicious attacks in interpersonal relations. Andrae had already called me aside and warned me, "You must be strong and remain focused. Do not be threatened by anyone. I do not have a relationship with anyone here, so no one should bother or look at you as a threat. Yes, some women used to be interested in me, but by now, they must have outgrown that expectation, I believe." He mentioned them by name. He also showed me photos of the ladies whom he had dated before. He would show me their photos and then describe the kind of relationship that he had with them and how it had all ended. He went out of his way to show me that I had no competition in my relationship with him. He had to prepare me because the atmosphere was rough, and I witnessed it when I traveled with women from his church to Houston, Texas, for the *Woman Thou Art Loosed Convention.* Instead of attending the conference, there was a special session held in the hotel where we were booked to break me down. I heard words that are hard to repeat coming from the mouths of believers. The bone of contention was why would a person of the status of Andrae be interested in a person like me from Africa. It was too dark to be near him.

Black-on-black prejudice is rife among both black people in Africa, and those in the diaspora who came through slavery. Some members of Andrae's church feared that his association with me would devalue his status. Andrae was happy to have me. He would repeat my name so many times in a sentence to drive the point of his endearment of me. I did not question his love for me, but he did not perceive the viciousness of the opposition to the relations. He would cook and serve me personally while other guests were told to serve themselves. He was eager to settle down when I came into his life, but Satan had a narrative that he wanted the world to believe about Andrae Crouch. I realized that the church as we know it has people who have passed the belief that God speaks and that what He says should be obeyed. To those people, God has to say what people want, or else they will not believe or obey Him. I would ask people whom I knew from Africa to pray for me, but somehow, they were noncommittal because many of them did not want me to be with Andrae. It was a shameful display of immaturity as I looked back. As a race, we black people are sometimes driven by envy and immediate gratification. Very few of us think of tomorrow intending to invest in it. However, God has people who are faithful to him, and Andrae was one such person, as God revealed it to me. Still, Satan was hard after him, trying at every opportunity to superimpose a narrative contrary to who Andrae was. It was Satan himself who was using people to fight Andrae and me from being married so that he would disparage Andrae. I am not saying that Andrae Crouch was perfect, but I know that he was very godly, and God vouched for him. That man wanted to get married so much. Still, Satan fought it so badly that without any revelation of the magnitude of the battle involved, people around him became instruments of sabotage instead of vision carriers. Well, that was a costly loss for Zimbabwe, too, because God wanted to raise the capacity of many in the gospel music industry through Andrae for a season. I saw him work with some gospel musicians from Africa, like Ohemaa Mercy and others, coaching them on how to handle concerts and live performances, which helped build their capacity from learning from a legend. Andrae Crouch lived a holy life, and you could learn a lot by being near him in terms of how to handle criticism, the whole art of performance, and serving God genuinely. That kind of information is a gold mine for an upcoming gospel music artist who may not know how hard it is to navigate an industry that has many challenges. This is the whole essence of apostleship. Why would God want Christians involved in the economic turnaround of a nation? It is because no ordinary person without an apostolic mandate could challenge the Njelele shrine system with success. God had a battle plan for the economic revival of the nation, but the church was napping, and some of its members fought the very thing that was a gateway to their progress. As I write this book, the church in Zimbabwe is going through a very challenging time because it has lacked perception at strategic moments of visitation in some instances. The music industry in Zimbabwe still did well despite all the negative developments that blocked Andrae from working with local gospel artists. Still, some of the young people had to grope in the difficult environment without the mentoring that was needed to make them established as worshippers in the house of God. Casualties of faulty character, lack of sanctification, and serving God for who He is and not what God can do for them in providing money for luxurious living. I watch with so much pain when I see the struggles of some people in the music industry in Zimbabwe because leaders look out for themselves and not the wellbeing of others. Yet the same people in the church are quick to blame politicians for the same things they have not overcome.

One of the people from Andrae's church came to confess what he had done against me and Andrae. "When we realized that pastor Andrae was serious about you in a way that he had not demonstrated before, some of us in the church gathered together and prayed against the relationship. We did not want him to marry you." The man was not the only one who confessed, several people apologized for their role in trying to destroy my life. Others left the church because they were hopeful that their pastor was going to be married, and that would bring dignity to the local assembly. I understood the man during his confession and apology, but I reminded him that what he and his team had done was witchcraft prayer. They saw an enemy in what God was doing, and they questioned it. They seemed to know better than God what their pastor needed to do while controlling every move. They were not bluffing in their prayers. They released a spirit of death as mentioned in 1 John 3:14-18

14 We know that we have passed from death unto life, because we love the brethren. He that loveth not his brother abides in death.

15 Whosoever hateth his brother is a murderer: and ye know that no murderer hath eternal life abiding in him.

16 at this moment, perceive we the love of God because he laid down his life for us: we ought to lay down our lives for the brethren.

17 But whoso hath this world's good, and seeth his brother has the need, and shutteth up his bowels of compassion from him, how dwelleth the love of God in him?

18 *My little children, let us not love in word, neither in tongue; but indeed and truth.*
I nearly lost my life at the hands of believers. This is the plague that has entered the church of Jesus Christ.

These are practices that are now common in the body of Christ. For a long season, my fight was against other believers to do the will of God. God the Father delights to give us the kingdom, but how can He do that when we still exhibit childish ways in the body of Christ? When I kept working in such a place full of adversity, the Lord Jesus told me that such behavior is called "Laying down your life for the brethren because that is what Jesus Christ did- John 15:13. *Greater love has no one than this: to lay down one's life for one's friends.* God had called me to lay down my life for others. I had no clue what the practical experience of that verse felt like until the time I worked with Andrae Crouch. The concept of 'Greater Love' is a missing ingredient in the church. You cannot lay down your life for others without pain because when you lay your life down, friends trample on it like a doormat. If you complain, you are missing an important ingredient of greater love. It is called dying to self. Therefore when people trample on you like you are a doormat, you will not feel it because you are dead to yourself. If you do, then you are missing what greater love is about. The Lord Jesus Himself came to teach me that, and only then could I forgive and start the healing process. I have never heard any pastor talk about the concept of greater love than that.

    I also learned that the environment of a local church could hurt the attitude of believers who attend there. Some believers are blinded to what God is doing because they focus on the small agendas that seek to make themselves look big without seeking God. This is not only in the church. I have experienced that attitude of being self-serving even with national resources that are meant for the majority of citizens. In Zimbabwe, that attitude has been shaped by the national deity and its henchmen to the extent that the average Zimbabwean personality is so heavily influenced in the day to day living by idolatry that many of the church leaders fight God instead of submitting to His purpose and plan. The attitudes of competition and jealousy are so characteristic of the church in Zimbabwe, to the extent that God told me not to share what He was doing in my life with any interested person. Some pastors from Africa get angry when you mention African

Americans because they do not believe that they are the same people as them. As a people, we do not see God's grand plan for humanity.

I was amazed to hear God tell me that *"The Pan African leadership is shifting from Africa to African Americans."* God had earmarked Eddie Long for that purpose. Still, he lacked the character to handle the office. According to God, Eddie Long received that mantle from Robert Mugabe of Zimbabwe. Now I wonder if that mantle has been received by another person in the African American community with the character to handle the office according to God's standard when Eddie Long could not. If not, black people are groping in the dark without divinely appointed people to lead in the governance arena this season.

To sum up my assignment to Andrae Crouch, I can say that I nearly lost my life in the eleven years of intercession for him. It was a battle for years. I had never engaged in that kind of warfare intercession before. As I stood in the gap for Andrae, I realized that some of the attacks directed at him were hitting me in the place of intercession. Intercession has levels. Some of it is very dangerous, and you must be called and ordained by God to do it. It is like the difference between the Marine Corps and regular soldiers. The Lord told me at the start of the mission that *"You have never walked this way before"* Joshua 3:4. I was clueless about spiritual warfare. What I had done at ZISCO and the national broadcaster paled compared to what I encountered in the San Fernando Valley. With time, I gathered that a highly esteemed person like Andrae Crouch was also attacked by heavyweights of the kingdom of darkness.

Satan had hoped that if he harassed me enough, then I would pack and go back to Zimbabwe. I could not do that because it was heaven itself that had ordained me for the mission. I was prepared to die in it if there was no other way out, and I would not have been the first one to perish in the mission field. God in His mercy spared my life. The end of the assignment was as early as 2006, but I was not released to move on until 2013. In July 2006, I heard a loud sound of a herald proclaiming Revelation 21. It was like the sound of the shofar that broke the silence of the morning.

1 And I saw a new heaven and a new earth: for the first heaven and the first earth were passed away; and there was no more sea.

2 And I John saw the holy city, new Jerusalem, coming down from God out of heaven, prepared as a bride adorned for her husband.

3 And I heard a great voice out of heaven saying, Behold, the tabernacle of God is with men, and he will dwell with them, and they shall be his people, and God himself shall be with them, and be their God.

4 And God shall wipe away all tears from their eyes; and there shall be no more death, neither sorrow, nor crying, neither shall there be any more pain: for the former things are passed away.

5 And he that sat upon the throne said, Behold, I make all things new. And he said unto me, Write: for these words are true and faithful.

6 And he said unto me, It is done. I am Alpha and Omega, the beginning and the end. I will give him a thirst of the fountain of the water of life freely.

7 He that overcomes shall inherit all things, and I will be his God, and he shall be my son.

When the proclamation was made, the voice said, "*Now get up and go back to San Fernando Valley, and tell Kenny Cook to give you a job*" When that happened, I was in Riverside with barely a place that I could call home. I was instructed to avoid looking for a job for four years, and then suddenly, I had a specific place where I was supposed to go and work.

I learned a valuable lesson from the eleven years that Andrae was being fought by a stronghold called the spiritual host of wickedness in high places mentioned in

Ephesians 6. As a human being, I could not directly engage that power because that is above my level as a mortal. I had to cry to the Lord for mercy until He intervened. That crying took more than a decade. Then God gave me a blueprint on how He would intervene to end the attacks on Andrae Crouch. He said to me, *"Go join the choir, and you will see what I will do"* When you work with God, He regards you as an important partner, so I obeyed and joined the choir. I saw God intervene amazingly. God was also gracious to point out that we were dealing with a stronghold called a Spiritual host of wickedness in High places. It was a decade of high-level warfare. Only God can handle the intensity of the battle that I witnessed around Andrae Crouch. As with any divine assignment, it has a beginning and an end. One day, the assignment ended just like that. The things of God have no set pattern. All you do is obey and be ready for change at any minute. You do not belong to yourself but to Him. Very sorry for people who easily attach to environments because God is attached to His purpose, and those who serve Him should answer when He calls. The timing also is never definite, but God is the most organized employer that I have ever worked for, as long as I conform to His schedule.

Chapter 12
Focus on praying for Zimbabwe

I got settled in interceding for Andrae Crouch so that he would live long enough to fulfill his calling. From the night that Satan appeared in my bedroom in Africa, contesting the prospect of my marriage to Andrae Crouch, in what I later understood as a courtroom session of heaven, God had followed that incident with more definite instructions. His assignment for me was to pray for Andrae Crouch so that he would not die before his time. If Andrae had died any sooner, then part of Andrae's mandate to 'connect generations' would not have come to pass. In the following conversations after the bedroom encounter, God did not mention the issue of marriage per se but told me that I was a gift to Andrae and his church.

I realized that I had been allowed to be in the courtroom of heaven, where I heard Satan contest the plan of God. However, Satan did not mention the details behind his spirited contest of God's plan for us, except to say that Andrae Crouch deserved to die and that he was not qualified to marry me. Other people were praying during that season, but the difference between me and them was that I was mandated by God to do the intercession. That meant that if Andrae died before he could fulfill his mandate, then it meant that I would have failed in my God-mandated assignment. I was not interceding for Andrae because I was popular with him or other people around him. No. It was a very challenging environment. The reason why the assignment was challenging was so that I could give up, and that would have made sense. Satan's hand was behind all the hardships that I faced because he had a duty to prove God wrong in selecting me for the assignment. He even appeared to me again many times while I was in California, telling me that he would fight me until I returned to Africa. It was so hard and traumatizing that I begged God to let me go back, but I knew that going back was not an option. No one should ever quit on an assignment because it is hard.

One can only quit when God says it is done. The enemy's trap was to sabotage the assignment to pray for Andrae through his initial romantic gesture toward me. I could have been bitter and moved away. Without revelation, such a move would have been sensible to make. However, I got revelation through the help of the Holy Spirit to understand that having a romantic relationship with Andrae Crouch was a beneficiary of the assignment if it had materialized to the point of marriage. Still, the assignment pertained to the divine purpose of God of ensuring that enough intercession was made for Andrae so that the will of God would not fail. I was called by God to minister to Andrae Crouch as a servant of God. Andrae's attitude, as well as that of those around him, was not a determining factor of my level of obedience to God. I had one master, God, who determined what I should do from time to time. The power of intercession opens up heavenly realms to broaden one's knowledge about what is going on in the world. It was in that state that God began to talk to me about Zimbabwe. In intercession, there are no boundaries about what areas an intercessor should cover in prayer and what they should

not. While praying for Andrae and America, God brought up Zimbabwe in the mix.
God began to train me on how He wanted me to carry out the assignment of praying for Zimbabwe. It was all new. God is more than an academic, as I gathered later on. Sometimes, God gives you a phrase and then expects you to use that phrase to research the subject matter that He tells you until you find the facts and understand what He is saying. Information is not just dished out because God wants diligence and resourcefulness from all of us.
In 2007, God told me that He wanted me to engage in prophetic writing. I realized that God had sent me to work as a journalist before so that I would use journalistic skills to write prophetically. I say this because some of the things that you read about in these pages were given to me by God as I engaged in intercession. Regarding Zimbabwe, God posed a question to me. "Who built Great Zimbabwe?" My answer was quick. I said, "The Rozvi" God went on, "If you check in the Rozvi praise poetry, do you find any reference to Great Zimbabwe or anything that associates that tribe with the monuments." In my High School and undergraduate studies, I studied *Nduri dzenhango dzemu Zimbabwe by J. Haasbroek,*

1980, which gave me an insight into Shona praise poetry. When God asked me the question, I was aware of the subject matter of praise poetry. Then God went on to say, "If the achievements of a tribe are encapsulated in their praise poetry or *chidawo,* why would the Rozvi leave out such an important aspect of their history?" God went on to ask me another question. "Why is their founder Nyatsimbe Mutota called Mwenye- Mutapa? That title describes his military prowess right? Mwenye-Mutapa means the one who conquered VaMwenye." Having grown up in the Mberengwa district of the Midlands Province, I always heard elders in the village refer to VaRemba people as VaMwenye. Not only that, my grade six teacher struggled one day over the name *Mwenye-Mutapa* because he was aware of VaRemba people as VaMwenye, and why was that name associated with the founding father of the Rozvi empire? I watched my teacher agonize over that name, as he knew that surrounding villages were inhabited by VaMwenye. He wondered why the two names were connected. Eventually, we went on with the lesson, but the bewilderment on my teacher's face stuck with me for years. It was not a surprise when the same issue came up in my conversation with God in America. God made me aware that Mwenye- Mutapa won the title because he conquered a people called VaMwenye, which became his honorific title. God explained that if Nyatsimbe Mutota defeated VaMwenye, then who were VaMwenye? If Mutota defeated VaMwenye, did he take over an existing state or founded one? Moreover, God asked me another question. "Why are Mutota's people called VaRozvi-Destroyers? Does that not imply that the Mutapa Kingdom was born out of military strength, which destroyed other people? Check those facts because they have to do with the country's foundation." As time went on, the Holy Spirit began to pronounce the name "Indiana Jones." I kept repeating the name until the Holy Spirit added another word, *Indiana Jones Movie."* The Holy Spirit told me that what He was giving me to write about Zimbabwe had something to do with the Indiana Jones Movie. When I researched further, I realized that the Indiana Jones movie in question had the title *Raiders of the Lost Ark*. From that conversation, I gathered that God had a vested interest in the affairs of Zimbabwe that have to do with His kingdom in a much deeper way which the people of Zimbabwe need to understand.

Zimbabwe

God began to make me understand that my rape experience and physical abuse were directly connected to a system of worship that is venerated in Zimbabwe. For clarity, vaMwenye or VaRemba are black people who migrated from Yemen and settled in present-day Zimbabwe. In Yemen, they came from a place called Senna, then moved to Mozambique, where they established what they called Senna 2. From Senna 2, they moved to Gokomere, where they established Sena 3. History records that there was a culture that is supported by archeological excavations that prove that there once existed what is called the Gokomere culture. From Gokomere, they moved to present-day Messina or Musina in South Africa.

The main problem that Zimbabwe faces is **idolatry-** the worship of a physical object as a god. Within that idolatry are encapsulated practices that destroy the foundations of people's lives. The deities of Zimbabwe require, as part of their worship, engagements in acts like incest, the desecration of virgins, orgies, and the general destruction of the moral fiber of a group of people. These acts are connected to the rampant problem of rape of minors. The people who engage in these acts are performing a ritual to a deity, and as such, they will not stop as long as their covenant with the deity subsists. Once such a system of worship is initiated by an individual, even their descendants are drawn into the practice from generation to generation because we identify with whom we worship. This also goes for ritual murders in families where you find an innocent child engaging in murder. The child may be innocent, but the requirement of the deity that the family worships is that blood should be shed at a particular point in time. The child is part of the system of worship under the choices made by the parents, so the commission of murder is part of the initiation ritual into the family system of worship through not just sin but iniquity. Iniquity in Hebrew is "Avon" and means "to bend, twist, distort," so iniquities are bending, twisting, or distorting the law of God's Word to different degrees worthy of punishment. Iniquity is certainly a violation of the right or duty that mankind is under an obligation to do. Iniquity increases in strength

and vileness from generation to generation. This may shed light on the murder cases reported even in the diaspora among some Zimbabweans because what we worship is a part of us, and it follows us wherever we go. These idolatrous and iniquitous practices have an impact on marriages, too, because every relationship is governed by the deity whom the family has established ties with. Yes, we call ourselves Christians in Zimbabwe. Still, if, in our background, there are some covenants made with a spiritual being in the bloodline, we cannot wish away such a connection because it is governed by decrees that are legal in the spirit, which have to be enforced. They have to invoke the superior law of God through the blood of Jesus Christ to override the laws instituted by the covenant with a deity. Without such a move, people can go to church on Sunday, but the God of heaven is not their God. They are being ruled by another set of laws that are contrary to what the Bible says. This is why Jesus points out in Matthew 7: 21-23, "*Not everyone that saith unto me, Lord, Lord, shall enter into the kingdom of heaven; but he that doeth the will of my Father which is in heaven.*
22 *Many will say to me on that day, Lord, Lord, have we not prophesied in thy name? and in thy name have*

cast out devils? and in thy name done many wonderful works?
23 *And then will I profess unto them, I never knew you: depart from me, ye that work iniquity."*

That same practice applies to the practice of witchcraft too. Derek Prince defines witchcraft as the religion of a fallen race. Anyone practicing witchcraft is, in other words declaring that he or she is still existing in the fallen nature of Adam and needs redemption. Witchcraft cannot be mixed with worshiping the God of heaven with success because it is an abomination. In Zimbabwe, some pass on witchcraft as an heirloom, meaning that covenants with deities of the craft bind the people involved in a type of behavior and habits that define them as practitioners of the trade. However, such people cannot inherit the kingdom of God and His Christ.

In Zimbabwe, worshiping the national deity at the Njelele shrine qualifies the nation as a nation of idolaters. It means that by bowing down to that deity as a nation, we cannot turn around and say rape is bad witchcraft is bad because these are how the national deity is worshipped. The style of worship has thrown beautiful people into serious bondage and caused untold suffering. It is on that basis that, as a nation, Zimbabwe cannot bribe God by declaring itself as a Christian nation while the shrine of Njelele and the statue of Nehanda are towering in its background. God is not mocked like that. God is calling for repentance by the people of Zimbabwe and the leadership from idolatry. I am not talking of repenting from present behavior because what we see now is iniquity. Still, the sins of idolatry that were committed by previous generations are the ones that we have received, and we are reaping the evil fruit of what our fathers did. They replaced God with totems. People are happier to identify with a totem than with God. That is an expression of idolatry.

The second part that God mentioned indirectly to me has to do with the Ark of the Covenant. I need to learn more detail about that. All that I heard was that in talking about Zimbabwe, there was an underlying issue that had something to do with the history of Zimbabwe. The issue was connected to the Indiana Jones movie. He said, "Do you know what you are writing has something to do with the Indiana Jones Movie? At that time, I did not know what the Indiana Jones Movie was about. When I found the information, I learned that it was about *The Raiders of the Lost Ark*. God did not elaborate on it but around the same time, I gathered that Tudor Parfit, a British Sociologist, had found an encasement of the Ark Of the Covenant in the Museum of Science in Zimbabwe. My focus was to follow the guidance of the Holy Spirit as I prayed for Zimbabwe. I came to realize that when God was asking me about silent aspects of history, like how the Rozvi got the name Rozvi-Destroyer, it was to draw my attention to the point that history may have omitted a crucial part of history that includes a group of people called VaMwenye as major players in the building of the nation of Zimbabwe. If there is anything like that, then the issue of the Ark of the Covenant becomes relevant to the history of Zimbabwe. When one looks at the term VaMwenye, concerning the evolution of language, local people in Southern Africa may have pronounced the term Yemenite in an adulterated manner, ending up with the term Mwenye. Could VaMwenye have something to do with the lost Ark of the Covenant? I would say that there is a greater possibility. Even a high-ranking Zimbabwean politician once boasted in the company of trusted friends that "Yes, Zimbabwe has the Ark of the Covenant" The catch in going all out to verify that postulation of the possibility of the presence of the Ark from a political standpoint, means that there will be a complete overhaul of power dynamics in the country. It may be convenient to let sleeping dogs lie about that matter, but God relishes talking about it. When God talks about a matter, it means that the season of reality from His standpoint has come, and no one can stop such a process.

God wants to bring an end to idolatry in Zimbabwe. He will judge righteously. God has an issue with his glory being shared with deities that are currently venerated in Zimbabwe if it is indeed true that His Ark is in the same place..

Psalm 149: 4 For the Lord taketh pleasure in his people: he will beautify the meek with salvation.
Psalm 149: 5-9 Let the saints be joyful in glory: let them sing aloud upon their beds.
6 Let the high praises of God be in their mouth, and a two-edged sword in their hand;
7 To execute vengeance upon the heathen and punishments upon the people;
8 To bind their kings with chains and their nobles with fetters of iron;
9 To execute upon them the judgment written:
This honor has all his saints. Praise ye the Lord.

Chapter 13
Powers holding Zimbabwe down

Since the time that I was delivered from marine spirits and the dedication of my life to the kingdom of darkness made by my family, I have focused on helping other women to get the freedom that I received from God. Many women and men have been set free through the power of God.

In 2020, God was specific about Zimbabwe, indicating that the forty years in the wilderness are complete. In other words, like Israel, Zimbabwe went through a difficult forty-year journey because our leaders did not give Him the glory during the war of liberation and after independence.

I had the chance to help a young Zimbabwean woman living abroad. She was having a lot of demonic afflictions. I picked her as an example because of what happened during her deliverance experience.

The deliverance was in phases. The first time, she was a slave to members of her family who, because of her intelligence, wanted to use her brain through satanic manipulation to their advantage. What manifested through that girl were not demons but human spirits astral projecting and speaking through the girl. One of the human spirits was her uncle, brother to her mother, an elder in a Pentecostal church. He confessed that he had been using the girl for ritual sex. He was appearing to her, having sex with her but disguised as another person. The sexual encounters had been going on for a long time, and by the time of her deliverance, the girl had become her uncle's wife or concubine. After disconnecting the uncle, then the grandmother from her mother's side manifested also. The grandmother is alive, and when she manifests, she is very angry that her granddaughter thinks she is so special that she cannot come and join other family members in eating human flesh. She wants her granddaughter to be a witch.

Next came an aunt from the dad's side of the family, in the human spirit form as well, and she vowed that she was determined to kill the girl. The aunt pointed out that if the girl sets foot in Zimbabwe, she will kill her. The aunt confessed that she is a high priestess of a coven somewhere in Mashonaland Central. Lastly came a spirit that confessed that it came from the waters. The spirit claimed that the girl belonged to the marine kingdom, but her prayers were interfering with her relations with that kingdom. The mermaid spirit confessed that it had offered the girl 197 million dollars, but she refused to accept it, choosing to align with the plan of God for her life. The girl was supposed to receive the money and take on the responsibility of caring for cowrie shells under the water. That spirit disclosed what was happening in the girl's family that was supposed to be a secret. Cowrie shells were once used as a form of currency in some cultures. The marine kingdom still holds them with value to the point of wanting to enslave humans who will be in charge of keeping them.

The next phase of the deliverance was after her marriage. As a newly married couple, they encountered problems with Erectile Dysfunction- ED. That is strange for people who are young and never engage in behaviors that could cause that kind of problem. However, whenever marine spirits interfere with marriage, one of the problems that they cause is ED. This is because marine spirits want to destroy marriages, and they use every arsenal they have to sabotage the marriage. Some subversive activities caused by marine spirits can be distortion or contortion of a woman's face so that she either scares the husband or appears undesirable to the husband. Other attacks by the same spirits can emasculate the husband that he takes the role of the wife, and the wife becomes the man- role reversal. The marine spirit manifested in the first deliverance confessed that we had sliced its private parts by the sword of the spirit, the word of God. The spirit protested that its penis had been sliced by our weapons. The spirit was talking so fast, trying to distract us from casting it out, but God gave us the grace to have the sister delivered. Demons are vile, so they use vile language. The same applies to people who use vile language; It is a manifestation of a spirit in them that is demonic. After the initial deliverance, the girl was able to get married. Our team engaged the young lady in a deliverance prayer again when new problems with her life and marriage emerged. and without hesitation, an arrogant demon manifested again. It identified itself as the Queen of the Indian Ocean. As a territorial spirit, it was resistant because it is used to control. It was indignant and said, " I am the Queen of the Indian Ocean. I rule Zimbabwe from the highest office to the man on the street. Nehanda, and mapostora are ours. I am the one who made the church in Zimbabwe lukewarm. I made it cold, there is nothing left. There is no power anymore because I made it cold. There is nothing, it is dead. You are casting me out! How did you escape me because I am in control?" The demon was stubborn and refused to go until we read Revelation 18, which reminds the kingdom of darkness of its ultimate end. Satan and all the demons do not want to hear of their end in the lake of fire. When we read those scriptures, it left.

When you look at the flow of the rivers, they all connect to the Indian Ocean. Spiritually, it is like bringing all their wealth and any substance to present it to the one who rules the Ocean. We may have the shrine at Njelele, but that is just the entry point into the ocean waters. All of the rivers in Zimbabwe pay homage to the

Indian Ocean. In other words, all the river gods worshiped by different tribes and groups submitted to the Indian Ocean. It is a riverine system that uses marine powers to control the living, as well as interact with them.

Revelation 18 talks of the judgment of Babylon the Great to make us know that it is a system that networks the whole world, and wherever river gods are venerated, it means the system of Babylon is the object of worship.

Deuteronomy 18: 10-13

There shall not be found among you anyone that maketh his son or his daughter to pass through the fire, or that useth divination, or an observer of times, or an enchanter, or a witch; Or a charmer, or a consulter with familiar spirits, or a wizard, or a necromancer.

For all that do these things are an abomination unto the LORD: and because of these abominations, the LORD thy God doth drive them out from before thee.

Thou shalt be perfect with the LORD thy God. God is sovereign in all His ways and does not share His glory with anyone or anything else.

As I write this text, it is at the end of May 31, 2020. It is slightly over a month after Zimbabwe celebrated 40 years of independence from colonial rule. Forty years was the time that Israel spent in the wilderness facing various types of trials as well as tests, and a lot of the flaws that they had as a nation or individuals were revealed in that time of trial. Biblically, 40 represents a set period of testing, trial, or probation and the completion of such processing. It has been very important for me to draw parallels between the nation of Israel in its 40-year journey and the journey of Zimbabwe in its 40-year period after colonial domination. Israel was coming out of slavery as they started the wilderness journey. Zimbabwe came out of colonial domination and started a promising journey of self-rule. One cannot fail to share the excitement of both nations as the euphoria of freedom filled the atmosphere of the two nations. One cannot fail to note the trauma of the years of backbreaking oppression and enslavement the two nations were emerging from. Another glaring fact is the inexperience in self-rule. In the case of Israel, the fear of possible capture and enslavement again almost became a reality by the Red Sea.

Exodus 14: 10-15 10 And when Pharaoh drew nigh, the children of Israel lifted their eyes, and, behold, the Egyptians marched after them; and they were sore afraid: and the children of Israel cried out unto the LORD.
And they said unto Moses, Because there were no graves in Egypt, hast thou has taken us away to die in the wilderness? Wherefore hast thou dealt thus with us, to carry us out of Egypt?
Is not this the word that we did tell thee in Egypt, saying, Let us alone, that we may serve the Egyptians? For it had been better for us to serve the Egyptians than that we should die in the wilderness.
And Moses said unto the people, Fear ye not, stand still, and see the salvation of the LORD, *which he will shew to you today: for the Egyptians whom ye have seen today, ye shall see them again no more forever.*
14 The LORD *shall fight for you, and ye shall hold your peace.*
15 And the LORD *said unto Moses, Wherefore criest thou unto me? speak unto the children of Israel, that they go forward:*

The children of Israel did not have a fear of being captured and brought back to Egyptian rule, they regretted having listened to Moses in the first place because they viewed slavery as much easier than trying to escape and being captured again by Pharaoh because they had an understanding of the harshness of the punishment that would be meted out to them if they returned to Egypt. Immediately after leaving Egypt and at the first encounter with the challenge of recapture, the Israelites began to blame Moses for the challenge ahead of them, reminding him in Exodus 14: 12 Is not this the word that we did tell thee in Egypt, saying, Let us alone, that we may serve the Egyptians? For it had been better for us to serve the Egyptians than that we should die in the wilderness.

Faith is not something that the Israelites could not muster in the face of challenges, but the leadership of Moses and his faith in God's leading helped them to cross the Red Sea before Pharaoh's army could catch them. It takes unique qualities to lead a group of broken people ravaged by slavery or domination by a stronger group of people. If a leader of such people is as broken as they are, then trouble will beset such a journey. Another important issue is the source of counsel for a leader of broken people. Broken people want a leader to lead, and they follow because they are tired and nursing a lot of personal pain such that they have no time to look at other issues that affect them, choosing to let leadership do it. Still, when they perceive failure or danger, then they make wholesale blame on leadership. Even when Moses received instructions from God, the Israelites sometimes wanted quick-fix solutions to issues which led them into a life of murmuring and idolatry, which provoked the anger of God.

For Zimbabwe, the brokenness came from colonial domination and the liberation struggle. This is the group of people that Robert Mugabe led in the nation for nearly forty years of independence which was later carried over by Emerson Mnangagwa to complete the forty years. The people left leadership to politicians. Many of the earlier crops of politicians who were active in the decolonization of Africa had lived outside Africa for many years, where they interacted with many belief systems. One major influence was Freemasonry, which had been an active hand in the downfall of the Spanish empire. (Martin, Sanchez, 2015). Freemasonry championed democracy and change (rebuilding), which fueled the decolonization of Spanish colonies until they were left with the control of Cuba, and the Philippines archipelago by 1898. Decolonized nations also supported revolutionary movements, thereby spreading the influence of Freemasonry the world over.

The rebuilding of the nation of Zimbabwe could have meant something completely different to a freemason than it did to an average person on the streets of Zimbabwe. Doctrines serving dual meanings were infused with messages of hope that may have been based on initiations practiced in Freemasonry. Pierre Sanchez-Ferre, in his research on the *Freemasonic Synthesis and the origin of the Initiatic Tradition,* says, "But there is another light, another Sun that is hidden in the human being and is precisely the aim of the initiation, since it is not the man of the external senses who is initiated, but the solar, interior man, that who has a hidden. Sense that must be restored." In other words, the initiation process into a lodge is intended to capture the human soul. These were some of the messages that mingled with revolutionary messages calling for freedom from oppression. Without much understanding, many people aspiring to be independent received support for their struggle. Still, they also received bondage of the soul through the restoration of the soul's light based on ancient Egyptian practices. One cannot be certain if the political leaders understood whether what they espoused as restoration was nation-building or initiation into Freemasonry. Part of the revolutionary and post-independent messages was about returning to our traditions without any practical analysis of what was idolatrous and what was genuinely a historical practice upheld by a group of people to empower their identity. The indiscriminate acceptance of everything called tradition is problematic as some people equated God with their ancestors. In the case of Israel, Moses remained connected to God throughout the journey even if he got angry with the people and failed to follow instructions which caused him to fail to enter the promised land-Exodus 31:19. In Deuteronomy 32: 51-51, **God gives the reason that Moses was not permitted to enter the Promised Land: "This is because you broke faith with me in the presence of the Israelites at the waters of Meribah Kadesh in the Desert of Zin and because you did not uphold my holiness among the Israelites. Therefore, you will see the land only from a distance; you will not enter the land I am giving to the people of Israel." (NIV) God is tougher on leadership than He is with followers because what a leader does affects followers positively or negatively.**

In Zimbabwe, the advent of independence saw a return to ancestral worship both as a tradition and as well a reaction to or rebelling against Christianity which had been seen as the facilitator of the colonial domination that black people had endured for years before deciding to pick up arms in the liberation struggle for Zimbabwe. *Chivanhu* (a term that defines African traditional practice) was a redefinition of what the black people of Zimbabwe had upheld for centuries. The worship of ancestors and upholding of spirits that were believed to have led in the liberation struggle for Zimbabwe, like Nehanda, was venerated. The return to traditional practices was not a new thing, though. Even under foreign rule, black people maintained their traditional practices while they still professed to have converted to Christianity, a practice called syncretism. The Oxford dictionary defines syncretism as the amalgamation or attempted amalgamation of different religions, cultures, or schools of thought: This belief style endured for a long time under cover during colonial years and became overt after independence in 1980, with traditional ancestral worship taking the upper hand. Zimbabwean leadership facilitated a way of worship that was already in practice. It isn't easy to separate the practice of traditional ancestral worship from normal day-to-day living.

Consequently, anything that is said about the need to separate from idolatrous ways of worship in the Zimbabwean tradition cannot be done without appearing to attack the heart and soul of the existence of a black Zimbabwean. This enmeshment of ordinary traditional customs and spirituality has made it hard for a Zimbabwean to worship Yahweh or Jehovah without appearing like denigrating one's tradition. In many minds, traditional worship practices are the essence of worshiping Yahweh, yet it is not. Contradicting this belief system is like stripping a Zimbabwean of the essence of who they are because syncretism is part and parcel of daily life, and there is a lot of pride that shrouds these beliefs and practices. After independence in 1980, those who had fought for the liberation struggle seemed so distant from Christianity because they had fought and won against its institutions of the Whiteman's religion. This was a very subjective argument because Yahweh interacted with Africa well before the Whiteman arrived in Africa if the term white describes people of European descent. Africa had already hosted all the patriarchs of the house of Israel centuries before the advent of Jesus Christ. After Jesus Christ's death and resurrection, it is only during the missionary journeys of the time of Apostle Paul that Europe is evangelized in Acts 16: 9-10 And a vision appeared to Paul in the night; There stood a man of Macedonia, and prayed him, saying, Come over into Macedonia, and help us. And after he had seen the vision, immediately we endeavored to go into Macedonia, assuredly gathering that the Lord had called us to preach the gospel unto them. Present-day Macedonia includes Greece and southwestern parts of Bulgaria.

Political expediency gave credence to propaganda messages that crossed the sacred boundaries, dismissing God as a deity worshiped by people who lacked credibility and who had dispossessed African people in the country of their land and freedom, thereby depicting God as an avaricious deity. While such language promoted a political message, it put the nation in a place where people willingly accorded the power to their ancestors as the ones who masterminded their freedom. This was wrong because God is bigger than propaganda. As a nation, we reduced the God of the universe to an insignificant deity who is worshiped by people who do not understand the history of the nation. Yet God is a just God who rules with equity. He also declares that He is God by Himself and that there is no one else besides Him. In Exodus 20: 3, He says," You shall have no other gods before me." In our anger, we made decisions that put us on a collision course with the God of the universe as a nation.

When Moses spent 40 days and 40 nights in the mountain with God, the Israelites got impatient and made a decision: Exodus 32 :1 *And when the people saw that Moses delayed to come down out of the mount, the people gathered themselves together unto Aaron, and said unto him, Up, make us gods, which shall go before us; for as for this Moses, the man that brought us up out of the land of Egypt, we wot not what is become of him.*

The Israelites decided to change the pattern of the process of liberation. God had liberated them from oppression through the hand of Moses, but suddenly, they wanted gods of their own making to lead them. All of a sudden former slaves wanted to hold the reins of their freedom and not follow the One who had liberated them. They demeaned and dismissed the worth of Moses as the messenger of God, and they redefined Aaron's priesthood from a servant of God and priest to an idolater. All that seemed harmless to people who were determined to express their freedom. They failed to understand the power of spiritual boundaries and the consequences of breaking them nonchalantly.

Exodus 32: 2-7 And Aaron said unto them, *Break off the golden earrings, which are in the ears of your wives, of your sons, and your daughters, and bring them unto me.*

³ And all the people brake off the golden earrings in their ears and brought them unto Aaron.

⁴ And he received them at their hand, and fashioned it with a graving tool, after he had made it a molten calf: and they said, These be thy gods, O Israel, which brought thee up out of the land of Egypt.

⁵ And when Aaron saw it, he built an altar before it; Aaron made proclamation, and said, Tomorrow is a feast to the LORD.

⁶ And they rose early on the morrow, offered burnt offerings, and brought peace offerings, and the people sat down to eat and to drink and rose to play.

⁷ And the LORD said unto Moses, Go, get thee down; for thy people, which thou broughtest out of the land of Egypt, have corrupted themselves:

For the Israelites, God saw making a golden calf as an act of self-desecration(the people corrupted themselves). The Bible says in

Hebrews 13: 8 Jesus Christ is the same yesterday, today, and forever then, it means that God's standard would not be any different for all of humanity, Zimbabwe included.

Chapter 14
History and national destiny

For Zimbabweans, the anger towards colonialism and early missionary activities caused Christianity to be relegated to a secondary status in the system of worship after independence. There emerged an inability to separate the fallibility and machinations of men, even with a bible in their hands, from the omnipotence of God. Psalm 24: 1 says *The earth is the LORD's, and the fullness thereof; the world, and they that dwell therein.* At the end of the day, whether we decide to disown God or submit to Him, His supremacy is not changed.

The black leadership that came into power in 1980 when Zimbabwe became independent took the reins of power that were highly contested by the UDI government. No one ever examined the spiritual significance of a refusal to have a smooth handover-take-over process. Why was Rhodesia such a valued possession of the British and later the Unilateral Declaration of Independence government led by Ian Smith? Leadership or control is both physical and spiritual. The Rhodesia government never conceded that they lost the war to guerillas but were betrayed by the British government of Margaret Thatcher. On the other hand, the former liberation war guerillas rejoiced that they had won over the leadership of their country, albeit with stipulations from the British government, which regained its colonial control of Southern Rhodesia under the governorship of Lord Soames until a general election decided the winner. While ZANU PF won the election, the Lancaster House talks to end the Rhodesia Bush War guaranteed that 20 percent of seats in Parliament were to be reserved for whites. The other stipulation was that the black government that would take over if it won the election would not implement the land reform for the first ten years after independence. While these may appear like ordinary historical facts, the reluctance by the British to completely relinquish all control and leave the UDI government and the Bush fighters to settle matters internally left a spiritual open door that could be manipulated in any way. Is it possible to define the independence of a state with another state as prefect over it, as was the case with Zimbabwe and the British government?

As the nation witnessed over the first ten years of Zimbabwe's independence, there were baronesses, Lords, and chairs of the Commonwealth visiting Zimbabwe one after another. It was like Zimbabwe was independent but with British oversight. Soon after the expiration of that arrangement, the Zimbabwe government faced the challenges of land reform and subsequent sanctions as if to say that without British oversight, the black rule was a non-starter. This power play left both the UDI government and its ZANU PF counterpart united in the same boat of institutions with a rebellious streak, and hence both qualified to be slapped with sanctions.

Intercessors, this is a prayer point; to contend for the relinquishing of a spiritual stranglehold on Zimbabwe by its former colonizer. It has to be released from rituals that perpetuate this control. It's like a rebellious child who will continue to attract the rod until a decision to submit or contend for autonomy is achieved in the heavens. To corroborate this fact is the issue of the burial of kings in African culture. While the grave of the last king of the Ndebele, Lobengula Khumalo, is still being searched for, and others believe that it is in the northern part of Zimbabwe, no one can pinpoint where a prominent national leader was laid to rest in the land that he ruled, leaving the only grave that is venerated as well as holding kingly significance to be that of Cecil John Rhodes. Although that can be dismissed as insignificant, the truth is that Cecil Rhodes was buried as a king, but none of the African leaders of Zimbabwe hold the same significance.

To reinforce the prominence of Cecil Rhodes as king in Zimbabwe, historical facts are murky about the aftermath of the Pupu-Shangani battle between King Lobengula and his forces against the Shangani Patrol Force of the settler government on November 4, 1893, and what became of King Lobengula Khumalo. The battle took place while King Lobengula and part of his forces were fleeing north, as they fled from Bulawayo, which was burning, having been set on fire by forces of the British South Africa Company. The Shangani Patrol, under Major Alan Wilson, was sent into Shangani to scout the area ahead of Major Patrick Forbes's column, to locate the fleeing Ndebele King, and capture him. Although Lobengula was not captured, and Major Alan Wilson and his patrol unit perished at the hands of Lobengula's soldiers, the allusion to the possible admission of defeat by Lobengula to the settler forces, allegedly sent through messengers to Rhodes' forces implies that by that admission, King Lobengula died as a fugitive, thereby dethroning his claim to kingship, and kingly burial. It boggles the mind to think that the burial site of a king who ruled the Ndebele kingdom for twenty-five years remains a century-old mystery that cannot be resolved. There is no evidence that subsequent generations could point to the burial site of the ancient king of the Ndebele. Here is an example of the power of evidence. In the book of Joshua 4: 1-3, 19-24, Israel was finally crossing the Jordan River to enter Canaan: *And*

it came to pass, when all the people were clean passed over Jordan, that the Lord spake unto Joshua, saying,
2 *Take you twelve men out of the people, out of every tribe a man,*
3 *And command ye them, saying, Take you hence out of the midst of Jordan, out of the place where the priests' feet stood firm, twelve stones, and ye shall carry them over with you, and leave them in the lodging place, where ye shall lodge this night.*
19 *And the people came out of Jordan on the tenth day of the first month encamped in Gilgal, in the east border of Jericho.*
20 *And those twelve stones, which they took out of Jordan, did Joshua pitch in Gilgal.*
21 *And he spake unto the children of Israel, saying, When your children shall ask their fathers in time to come, saying, What mean these stones?*
22 *Then ye shall let your children know, saying, Israel came over this Jordan on dry land.*
23 *For the Lord your God dried up the waters of Jordan from before you until ye were passed over, as the Lord your God did to the Red sea, which he dried up from before us until we were gone over:*
24 *That all the people of the earth might know the hand of the Lord, that it is mighty: that ye might fear the Lord your God forever.*

Black Zimbabweans have no evidence that points to a living history of kingship among them because the only grave that speaks of the memories of kingship in the nation is that of Cecil Rhodes. Even the Rozvi have no site that can be referenced as a royal burial site. Does that dent a people's self-esteem? Yes, it does! Where is the evidence of royalty among the indigenous people of the area?

It can be argued that even the burial sites of Robert Mugabe and Joshua Nkomo do not carry the same status as that of Cecil Rhodes. Former president Robert Mugabe who ruled the country for nearly forty years, is buried at his homestead in Zvimba. In 1999, Joshua Nkomo has declared a National Hero and is buried in the National Heroes Acre in Harare. Does this mean anything spiritually? Yes! A lot! In other words, "Rhodesia will never die" and "Never in a thousand years will a black man rule Rhodesia" The power of words and the evidence that supports their meaning cannot be ignored when you look at the two statements above and their connection to the burial sites of Cecil Rhodes, Lobengula Khumalo, Joshua Nkomo, and Robert Mugabe.

Chapter 15
Idolatry
The acquisition of independence by black Zimbabweans was a dream come true, just like Israel entering the promised land of Canaan. It is the poor management of what God placed into the hands of both nations as a heritage that provoked the anger of God. The problem is the sin of idolatry. Idolatry is "image-worship or divine honor paid to any created object." (Easton's Bible Dictionary)

God instructed humanity through Israel to punish any nation that worships what He created because he created humanity for His pleasure.

Deuteronomy 18: 9-14 *When thou art come into the land which the LORD thy God giveth thee, thou shalt not learn to do after the abominations of those nations.*

10 There shall not be found among you anyone that maketh his son or his daughter to pass through the fire, or that useth divination, or an observer of times, or an enchanter, or a witch, 11 Or a charmer, or a consulter with familiar spirits, or a wizard, or a necromancer. 12 For all that do these things are an abomination unto the LORD: and because of these abominations, the LORD thy God doth drive them out from before thee.

13 Thou shalt be perfect with the LORD thy God. 14 For these nations, which thou shalt possess, hearkened unto observers of times, and diviners: but as for thee, the LORD thy God hath not suffered thee so to do

God is very clear in His dealings with Israel and the nations of Canaan that whenever there is idolatry, then judgment is certain. We encounter Moses under the instruction of the Almighty God, explaining to the Israelites that idolatrous ways had caused the Canaanites to be dispossessed of their land by God, and it was being given to Israel. However, Israel, on its part, needed to understand the revulsion that God has with pairing Him with idols that do not talk and are the work of man's hands. So Moses admonishes Israel while they are yet in the wilderness before crossing the Jordan into Canaan, that God does not expect them to follow Canaanite ways of making their children pass through the fire or practice divination, or an observer of times or an enchanter, or a witch (Deut. 18: 10). He lists in the above scriptures what God abhors in His relationship with humanity. Canaanites lost their land to Israel because of their ways of worship and not because they were not enlightened because some of them were descendants of giants referred to as men of renown. They had a sophisticated military with chariots of iron with walled cities, which are mentioned in *Numbers 13:26- 28. They went and came to Moses, and Aaron, and all the congregation of the children of Israel, unto the wilderness of Paran, to Kadesh; and brought back word unto them, and all the congregation, and shewed them the fruit of the land. 27 And they told him, and said, We came unto the land whither thou sentest us, and surely it floweth with milk and honey, and this is the fruit of it.*

28 Nevertheless, the strong people dwell in the land, and the cities are walled and very great: and we saw the children of Anak there.

The original tribes of Canaan were affluent people and every human standard, progressive. Yet their land was taken from them because of their ways of worship which contradicted God's expectations. In this case, it is easier to argue that God had not spoken to these tribes in the manner He had spoken to Israel, and as such, their punishment was harsh. However, Romans 1: 18-21 *For the wrath of God is revealed from heaven against all ungodliness and unrighteousness of men, who hold the truth in unrighteousness; 19 Because that may be known of God is manifest in them; for God hath shewed it unto them. 20 For the invisible things of him from the creation of the world are seen, being understood by the things that are made, even his eternal power and Godhead; so that they are without excuse: 21 Because that, when they knew God, they glorified him not as God, neither were thankful; but became vain in their imaginations, and their foolish heart was darkened.*

The nations of Canaan were aware of the existence of Almighty God. Still, something had happened in that part of the world that deceived humanity and led them astray, being seduced by sin and iniquity. As I mentioned earlier, the spies sent by Moses said that they had seen the sons of Anak. The Anakim/Anakites were a formidable race of giants, warlike people (Deuteronomy 2:10, 21; 9:2) who occupied the lands of southern Israel near Hebron before the arrival of the Israelites. Apart from the Canaanites, Amorites, Jebusites, Hivites, Girgashites, Perrizites, and Hittites, there were the descendants of the giants called the sons of Anak. These so-called pagan tribes of Canaan were full of pride and rebellion. Rebellion and pride were long-standing characteristics of these people, having their roots in Genesis 6:4

There were giants in the earth in those days; and also after that, when the sons of God came in unto the daughters of men, and they bore children to them, the same became mighty men which were of old, men of renown. King James Version (KJV). There was development and wealth in Canaan due to an illegal encounter that had taken place when angels engaged in sexual intercourse with the daughters of man (humans), and a breed called giants was born. It can be argued that in Zimbabwe, sexual intercourse between spirits and humans is commonplace, at the highest place of worship at Matobo, at the Njelele shrine. Although it may be hard to prove the genetic makeup of some of the humans born out of such unions, the practice itself qualifies the nation of Zimbabwe to be defined as idolatrous. There are some Canaanite practices in the nation that are defined as abominable before God.

The giants in Genesis 6 became famous and mighty in the war. God had not sanctioned that interaction of man and angels, and when it happened, the whole region was affected by the advent of these giants because they became influential beings. So, the rebellious streak that characterized the region on the arrival of Israel was not a new thing but something that had been going on for centuries. That rebellion provoked God to the point of deciding to cut off the tribes of Canaan by taking away land from them and giving it to Israel to introduce a godly way of worship. God can take away any land from any person or group without answering to anyone because Psalm 24: 1 says that *The earth is the Lord's and its fullness, the world, and they dwell therein.*

Consequently, the Israelites were instructed by God in the wilderness to separate themselves and to listen to His instructions. Exodus 23: 20-25 [20] *Behold, I send an Angel before thee, to keep thee in the way, and to bring thee into the place I have prepared.*²¹ *Beware of him, and obey his voice, provoke him not; for he will not pardon your transgressions: for my name is in him.*²² *But if thou shalt indeed obey his voice, and do all that I speak; then I will be an enemy unto thine enemies, and an adversary unto thine adversaries.*

²³ *For mine Angel shall go before thee, and bring thee in unto the Amorites, and the Hittites, and the Perizzites, and the Canaanites, the Hivites, and the Jebusites: and I will cut them off.* ²⁴ *Thou shalt not bow down to their gods, nor serve them, nor do after their works: but thou shalt utterly overthrow them, and quite break down their images.*

²⁵ *And ye shall serve the* LORD *your God, and he shall bless thy bread, and thy water; and I will take sickness away from the midst of thee.* The Bible says in 1 Samuel 15:23 (a, b), *For rebellion is as the sin of witchcraft, and stubbornness is as iniquity and idolatry.* For the Canaanites, a rebellion had not just been something that humans decided on but was of spiritual origin, with angelic beings getting involved sexually with humans against God's law and then that rebellion resulting in the physical manifestation of children called giants born out of those unions.

The Book of Enoch

The Book of Enoch sheds some light on this rebellion. I will quote chapter 68. However, all online versions of the book have chapter 68, which is chapter 69 in the hard copy, but the content is the same except for the chapter numbering. I decided to use online numbering. This chapter gives the names of the angels who rebelled and the secrets they revealed to humans against God's order.

1. After this judgment, they shall be astonished and irritated, for it shall be exhibited to the earth's inhabitants. 2. Behold the names of those angels. These are their names. The first of them is Semjaza; the second, Arstikapha: the third, Armen; the fourth, Kakabael; the fifth, Turel; the sixth, Rumyel; the seventh, Danyal; the eighth, Kael; the ninth, Barakel; the tenth, Azazel; the eleventh, Armers; the twelfth, Bataryal; the thirteenth, Basasael; the fourteenth, Ananel; the fifteenth, Turyal; the sixteenth, Simapiseel; the seventeenth, Yetarel; the eighteenth, Tumael; the nineteenth, Tarel; the twentieth, Rumel; the twenty-first, Azazyel.

3. These are the chiefs of their angels, and the names of the leaders of their hundreds, and the leaders of their fifties, and the leaders of their tens. 4. The name of the first is Yekun: he it was who seduced all the sons of the holy angels and causing them to descend on earth, led astray the offspring of men. 5. The name of the second is Kesabel, who pointed out evil counsel to the sons of the holy angels, and induced them to be corrupt their bodies by generating mankind. 6. The name of the third is Gadrel: he discovered every stroke of death to the children of men. 7. He seduced Eve; and discovered to the children of men the instruments of death, the coat of mail, the shield, and the sword for slaughter; every instrument of death to the children of men. 8. From his hand were these things derived to them who dwell upon the earth, from that period forever. 9. The name of the fourth is Penemue: he discovered to the children of men bitterness and sweetness; 10. And pointed out to them every secret of their wisdom. 11. He taught men to understand writing and ink and paper. 12. Therefore numerous have been those who have gone astray from every period of the world, even to this day. 13. For men were not born for this, thus with pen and ink to confirm their faith; 14. Since they were not created, except that, like the angels, they might remain righteous and pure. 15. Nor would death, which destroys everything, have affected them; 16. But by this, their knowledge they perish, and by this also its power consumes them. 17. The name of the fifth is Kasyade: he discovered to the children of men every wicked stroke of spirits and demons: 18. The stroke of the embryo in the womb, to diminish it; the stroke of the spirit by the bite of the serpent, and the stroke which is given in the mid-day by

the offspring of the serpent, the name of which is Tabaet. 19. This is the number of the Kesbel; the principal part of the oath which the Highest, dwelling in glory, revealed to the holy ones. 20. Its name is Beka. He spoke to holy Michael to discover the sacred name so that they might understand that secret name and thus remember the oath; and that those who pointed out every secret thing to the children of men might tremble at that name and oath. 21. This is the power of that oath; for powerful it is and strong. 22. And he established this oath of Akae by the instrumentality of the holy Michael. 23. These are the secrets of this oath, and by it were they confirmed. 24. Heaven was suspended by it before the world was made, forever.
25. By it has the earth been founded upon the flood, while from the concealed parts of the hills, the agitated waters proceed from the creation to the end of the world. 26. By this oath, the sea has been formed and the foundation of it. 27. During the period of its fury, he has established the sand against it, which continues unchanged forever; and by this oath, the abyss has been made strong; nor is it removable from its station forever and ever. 28. By this oath, the sun and moon complete their progress, never swerving from the command given to them forever and ever. 29. By this oath, the stars complete their progress; 30. And when their names are called, they return an answer forever and ever. 31. Thus, in the heavens take place the blowings of the winds: all

of them have breathings and affect a complete combination of breathings. 32. There, the treasures of thunder are kept, and the splendor of the lightning. 33. There are kept the treasures of hail and frost, the treasures of snow, rain, and dew. 34. All these confess and lie before the Lord of spirits. 35. They glorify with all their power of praise, and he sustains them in all that act of thanksgiving while they laud, glorify, and exalt the name of the Lord of spirits forever and ever. 36. And with them he establishes this oath, by which they and their paths are preserved; nor does their progress perish. 37. Great was their joy. 38. They were blessed, glorified, and exalted because the name of the Son of man was revealed to them. 39. He sat upon the throne of his glory, and the principal part of the judgment was assigned to him, the Son of man. Sinners shall disappear and perish from the face of the earth, while those who seduce them shall be bound with chains forever. 40. According to their ranks of corruption shall they be imprisoned, and all their works shall disappear from the face of the earth; nor thenceforward shall there be any to corrupt; for the Son of man has been seen, sitting on the throne of his glory. 41. Everything wicked shall disappear and depart before his face, and the word of the Son of man shall become powerful in the presence of the Lord of spirits. 42. This is the third parable of Enoch.

The act of rebellion by these angels caused humans to stray from their relationship with God. Once they were involved with these fallen beings, it appeared there was no going back until God judged them by dispossessing them of their land, giving it to the people who were in covenant with Him. So it is possible to lose one's heritage if the person is at cross-purposes with God's original plan. Enslavement is another consequence of rebellion against God. One thing to note is that for Canaanite tribes, their practices were their tradition, but God abhorred their way of worship. What were the Canaanite practices that infuriated God?

Chapter 16
Deities worshiped in Zimbabwe.

The Canaanites worshiped other gods. This is a great offense to God because He has made it clear that there should not be any other god to be worshiped besides Him. They engaged in temple prostitution which was thought to be a re-enactment of the sexual unions of the gods and goddesses. They engaged in child sacrifice. In examining the names and worship styles of these gods, one can find striking examples of Zimbabwean traditional worship. Unfortunately, when such issues arise, indigenous people feel like they are being undressed by all that makes them who they are. One cannot clothe oneself in idolatry and expect to succeed in any area of life. Many are made to feel inferior to the Bible standard, even those of other cultures, and resent that. Yet any culture no matter how superior it, may have to pass the standard God has prescribed, and if that standard is not met, then it does not cut. The standard of God is designed for mankind to have communion with Him, and that standard is standard. Let us have a look at the characteristics and styles of worship of some of the deities. Then later, it becomes easier to draw similarities between some African practices and that of Zimbabwe.

Ashtoreth: Asherah, or Ashtoreth, was the name of the chief female deity worshiped in ancient Syria, Phoenicia, and Canaan. Specifically, she was the female god of the Sidonians. The Phoenicians called her Astarte, the Assyrians worshiped her as Ishtar, and the Philistines had a temple of Asherah. The name and cult of the goddess were derived from Babylonia, where Ishtar represented the evening and morning stars and was accordingly androgynous (partly male and partly female) in origin. In Moab, Ashtoreth is identified with Chemosh.

Asherah was represented by a limbless tree trunk planted in the ground. The trunk was usually carved into a symbolic representation of the goddess. Because of the association with carved trees, the places of Asherah worship were commonly called "groves,"

Considered the moon goddess, Asherah was often presented as a consort or wife of Baal, the sun god. Asherah was also worshiped as the goddess of love and war and was sometimes linked with Anath, another Canaanite goddess. Worship of Asherah was noted for its sensuality and involved ritual prostitution. There are claims that virgins were sacrificed if they did not submit to the role of prostitution during worship ceremonies. The priests and priestesses of Asherah also practiced divination and fortune-telling.

In Deuteronomy 16: 21 God said, *"You shall not plant any tree as an Asherah beside the altar of the LORD your God that you shall make.*

In Babylonia and Assyria, Ishtar was the goddess of love and war. A Babylonian legend related how the descent of Ishtar into Hades in search of her dead husband, Tammuz, was followed by the cessation of marriage and birth in both earth and heaven. This deity was regarded as a type of female divinity, a personification of the productive principle in nature, and more especially, the mother and creatress of mankind whose worship in Babylonia was characterized by prostitution, and she was served with immoral rites by bands of men and women. In other areas, Ashteroth was worshiped as a woman with a tail of a fish, and in such cases, the fish became sacred to the deity. In Deuteronomy **23:18, God warns the Israelites that "** *You must not bring the earnings of a female prostitute or a male prostitute into the house of the LORD your God to pay any vow because the LORD your God detests them both. '*

Baal

Baal was the name of the supreme god worshiped in ancient Canaan and Phoenicia. The Israelites are faced with and embrace the worship of Baal after entering The Promised Land. The myth surrounding Baal was that he was the son of El, the chief God, and Asherah, the goddess of the sea, whose powers eclipsed those of his father, El, to make Baal supreme.

Baal defeated other deities like Yamm, the god of the sea, and Mot, the god of death and the underworld. Baal was a fertility god. The fertility was manifested in making the land produce abundantly in terms of harvests and enabling people to have children. The worship of Baal is adaptable to any region, like Baal Peor and Baal Berith, who were Baals of different areas. Baal's consorts were Ashtoreth, a fertility goddess associated with the stars, and Anath, a goddess of love and war. As the sun and storm god, Baal is depicted holding a lightning bolt with which he defeats his enemies to cause abundant harvests and make people have children.

    The reverberating themes characterizing the worship of Baal, Ashtoreth, and some of the Zimbabwean African traditional worship converge in practice.

    Zimbabwe has a hierarchy of traditional spiritual authority worshiped at the individual, family, tribal, regional, and national levels. Chiefs or kings have, from time immemorial, presided over matters of traditional worship. This makes chiefs custodians of the land, people, and spiritual worship. The chiefs own the land, but they also submit to Mulimo at Njelele. In other words, chiefs hold the land on behalf of the deity.

A poignant example of rituals that accompany the installation of a chief who is the ruler of a particular area as well as the custodian of the land on behalf of the spirits or ancestors was in a video clip of an area in Manicaland that circulated on social media. In that video, the individual who is going to be chief sits on a mat, and a traditional alcohol brew is poured on him, to the dancing and ululation of his subjects. Women simulate sexual intercourse with the man publicly in practice called *kunyengwa*. That aspect of the ceremony is x-rated. More of an orgy. This is a modern simulation of what used to happen in the past, according to those who know the tradition, and point out that in the past, the installation or death of a chief was marked by orgies or *nzveura* in which people at the ceremony slept with any woman or man available to the extent that some women would get pregnant at such ceremonies. If a married woman got impregnated, her husband could not put her away because the pregnancy came as a result of the fun at the chief's installation. The woman would not face any consequences for such infidelity. In other words, drunken orgies have a place in which they are allowed in Zimbabwean tradition in some parts of the country.

The installation of a chief went further regarding sexual encounters, as the chief would have an incestuous encounter with his daughter in the river or pool. This practice is called *Kupingapasi*.

These sexual practices are regarded as part of the ceremony during the death and installation ceremonies of chiefs but what is not explicit is that the practices are a way of worshipping deities of fertility and rain that make the land productive. It is clear that from the forms of worship of Baal and Ashteroth, our Zimbabwean traditional practices are akin to worshiping the deities. While it is regarded as mere tradition, those who profess to be Christians cannot partake of such practices not because they are pagans but worship other gods. The lack of understanding of why some of our traditions are forms of worship that spark conflicts with Christianity is because traditionalists feel that believers in Jesus Christ ostracize traditionalists without taking time to understand the meaning of what they do. On the other hand, Christians who do not understand the depth of meaning of some traditions double dip in Christian practice and traditional worship.

If a chief engages in drunken orgies and incestuous encounters in the river, it is important to understand that the river is where river gods or mermaids live. By performing such an act in the river, the chief would pay homage to the mermaid spirits or river gods. After such acts are done, the chief's leadership position is consolidated. In essence, the area under the chief's jurisdiction is offered to mermaid spirits through sexual activities that are vile. Also, the land under the chief's jurisdiction belongs to the spirits appeased at his inauguration. When the chief is regarded as the land owner, he does it on behalf of the spirits worshiped at his installation. Drunken orgies and incest are not acts done to appease ancestors but the ruling spirits of the area and nation.

Here comes the hypocrisy of some of the national laws of Zimbabwe. The judicial system punishes people for incestuous relations because it is illegal under the law, but chiefs do it at their inauguration. Why does the Zimbabwean judicial system regard incest as a crime? This is because it operates under the

Roman-Dutch law, which is Christian. As such, Christianity teaches that incest is not allowed by God because it is an abomination. So, whoever practices it is liable for punishment as a transgressor. However, tradition has some allowances for such practices.

This comes from the story of Lot and his daughters, who engaged in incest and raised a group of people called Moabites in Genesis 19:30-38- *Lot went up from Zoar and stayed in the mountains, and his two daughters with him; for he was afraid to stay in Zoar; and he stayed in a cave, he and his two daughters. Then the firstborn said to the younger, "Our father is old, and there is not a man on earth to come into us after the manner of the earth. Come, let us make our father drink wine, and let us lie with him that we may preserve our family through our father. So they made their father drink wine that night, and the firstborn went in and lay with her father, and he did not know when she lay down or when she arose. On the following day, the firstborn said to the younger, "Behold, I lay last night with my father; let us make him drink wine tonight also; then you go in and lie with him, that we may preserve our family through our father." So they made their father drink wine that night also, and the younger arose and lay with him, and he did not know when she lay down or when she arose. Thus both the daughters of Lot were with their father.*

The firstborn bore a son and called his name Moab; he is the father of the Moabites to this day. As for the younger, she also bore a son and called his name Ben-Ammi; he is the father of the sons of Ammon to this day.

Leviticus 18:6-12

'None of you shall approach any blood relative of his to uncover nakedness; I am the Lord. You shall not uncover the nakedness of your father, that is, the nakedness of your mother. She is your mother; you are not to uncover her nakedness. You shall not uncover the nakedness of your father's wife; it is your father's nakedness.

Genesis 38:16-18

The incest of Judah and Tamar

So he turned aside to her by the road and said, "Here now, let me come into you,"; for he did not know that she was his daughter-in-law. And she said, "What will you give me, that you may come to me?" He said, therefore, "I will send you a young goat from the flock." She said, moreover, "Will you give a pledge until you send it?" He said, "What pledge shall I give you?" And she said, "Your seal and your cord, and your staff that is in your hand." So he gave them to her and went into her, and she was conceived by him.

The twins born of this incestuous relationship were called Pharez and Zerah and were regarded as bastards because of how they were conceived. Deuteronomy 23:2 says - *A bastard shall not enter into the congregation of the LORD; even to his tenth generation shall he not enter into the congregation of the LORD. Ruth 4:18 gives us the descendants of Pharez until king David:* **18** *Now these are the generations of Pharez: Pharez begat Hezron, And Hezron begat Ram, and Ram begat Amminadab, And Amminadab, begat Nahshon, and Nahshon begat Salmon, And Salmon begat Boaz, and Boaz begat Obed, And Obed begat Jesse, and Jesse begat David.*

Due to incest, Israel went for ten generations without a king because the house of Judah, which was ordained to provide a king, had to wait for generations until the abomination was done away with. Jacob had pronounced the kingship of Judah while in Egypt when he blessed his sons in Genesis 49: 10 The *scepter will not depart from Judah,*

   nor the ruler's staff from between his feet,[c] until he to whom it belongs[d] shall come
   and the obedience of the nations shall be his.

There are ten generations between Judah, and David, according to the gospel of Matthew Chapter 1: 3-6

3 Judah, the father of Perez and Zerah, whose mother was Tamar,

Perez, the father of Hezron,
Hezron, the father of Ram,
4 *Ram, the father of Amminadab,*
Amminadab, the father of Nahshon,
Nahshon, the father of Salmon,
5 *Salmon, the father of Boaz, whose mother was Rahab,*
Boaz, the father of Obed, whose mother was Ruth,
Obed, the father of Jesse,
6 *and Jesse, the father of King David.*

The tenth generation emerged with king David. Israel was wondering about strictly adhering to the laws of God between Pharez and David, being ruled by Judges, and backsliding at times. When David came to power, he was a lover of God, worshiping until the skirts of his garments were seen. He brought back the Ark of the covenant and would have built a temple, but God stopped him because, as a soldier, David's hands were bloody. The responsibility to build a temple was taken over by his son Solomon. If Zimbabwe is caught up in this cause and effect of incest and banishment from the presence of God, then how many potential leaders were disqualified by God from assuming leadership positions because they carried a curse of a bastard without knowing it? The nation ends up with confusion over issues of leadership because the majority of people are reeling under a curse received generations before them at a drunken orgy. Purity and holiness before God do not exclude Zimbabweans. There are consequences for transgressing the laws of God. If this Old Testament principle is still in operation because sin is sin, whether in the old or new testament, then how clean are the seats of chiefs in the Zimbabwean leadership, and what is the fate of children born out of such encounters?

With such permissive behavior as drunken orgies and incest at official ceremonies, is it a wonder then that people would carry on the practices of wanton sexual behavior into their communities because they learned about it at their leader's installation ceremony?

Again, when infidelity is wantonly practiced, the perpetrators are castigated, but no one pays attention to the traditional systems which condone careless sexual behavior in society. The Roman-Dutch law-based judiciary has not examined the dissonance between traditional practices and their influence on peoples' behavior and how people are prosecuted for what tradition accepts.

So much has been said that is negative about the banning of traditional forms of worship with the advent of missionaries in Zimbabwe. No one has examined the true meaning of some of the practices of the time because they were contrary to the word of God and sometimes animistic.

Evil covenants

When a chief has sex in the pool in a river, he is not only performing a ritual but making covenants with river gods for power to rule. So the strength of a chief is based on covenants with spirits and not on his leadership skills. In the same vein, educated people in Zimbabwe do not believe that the knowledge that they have is sufficient. They believe that some ritual is needed for success to be achieved. The element of self-doubt among even some of the elite of Zimbabwe is steeped in traditional beliefs that emphasize ritual and not organization and diligence.

Matthew 7: 21-23 (KJV)

Not every one that saith unto me, Lord, Lord, shall enter into the kingdom of heaven; but he that doeth the will of my Father which is in heaven.

Many will say to me on that day, Lord, Lord, have we not prophesied in thy name? and in thy name have cast out devils? and in thy name have done many wonderful works?

And then will I profess unto them, I never knew you: depart from me, ye that work iniquity.
Why is iniquity such a deadly sin that attacks believers who may be serving God diligently? **Isaiah points out in Chapter 53: 5** *But he was wounded for our transgressions, he was bruised for our iniquities; The chastisement of our peace was upon him, and by his stripes, we are healed.*

Iniquity is sin at its worst. When missionaries came to Zimbabwe, they made converts who could have continued in drunken orgies, but the church's intervention helped the family structure. Not all traditional practices like incest practiced by a chief with his daughter or sister at his inauguration were healthy. After the war, traditional practices were given an upper hand, and Christian values were frowned upon. When we look back after forty years of independence, do we have pride as a nation that we have built durable systems as we ignored Christianity in favor of traditional worship? Zimbabwe has some of the sharpest brains in the world, yet our nation is crumbling. This is because, no matter how brilliant a human being can be, he or she cannot be at loggerheads with God and succeed.

By venerating traditional practices that many of the leaders understood fully, darkness was ushered into the nation, and it negatively impacted everything. It's not necessary to pat ourselves on our backs for being strong in a weak economy or blaming other nations for our predicament without taking most of the blame because iniquity is a force that has exerted its weight on Zimbabwe. Even in the face of all the difficulties, there is a stranglehold on forms of tradition that weaken our dreams and aspirations. When we see some of our citizens and those of other African nations or descent being sent home for sexual crimes from foreign countries, we also frown at their behavior. Still, we forget that we once told them that all our traditions are superior, but foreigners despise them. Some citizens force themselves on women in other nations and Zimbabwe, punishing them. Yet, at traditional ceremonies, these practices go on unabated. Not as simulations but as actual drunken orgies. Some fathers in business or some form of leadership believe that to be effective as a leader, they must engage in incestuous encounters with their daughters. Some mothers have sex with their sons. This is the power and impact of tradition on people, regardless of their level of education. Unfortunately, awareness of the areas of weakness in

Zimbabwean traditional practices has not been strong. As a result, citizens exhibit behaviors that align with what they believe to be tradition, and society punishes them for it. On the other hand, it is hard for leadership that once condoned tradition as sacrosanct while denigrating tenets of Christianity to renege on or admit that there are inherent weaknesses in some aspects of Zimbabwean traditions and some trends of inordinate and sexual encounters continue because the practice is part of a belief system.

During the liberation struggle, songs of propaganda harnessed Christian songs to put across their messages by replacing lyrics that gave glory to God and Jesus Christ with those that glorified their leaders. For example,

Taura neZANU, (Speak to ZANU}
Nhamo dzako dzose (All your problems)
Iyo ichakupindura… (It (ZANU) will answer you)
Ukataura neZANU uchakunda-a-a (If you speak to ZANU you will win)

This song was a translation of the Christian song:

Taura naJesu (Speak to Jesus Christ)
Nhamo dzako dzose (All your problems)
Iye achakupindura,. (He will answer you)

Ukataura naJesu uchakunda-a-a (If you speak to Jesus, you will win)

This is what the bible refers to in Romans 1: 21-25

21 Because that, when they knew God, they glorified him not as God, neither were thankful; but became vain in their imaginations, and their foolish heart was darkened.

22 Professing themselves to be wise, they became fools,

23 And changed the glory of the incorruptible God into an image made like to corruptible man, and birds, and four-footed beasts, and creeping things. 24 Wherefore God also gave them up to uncleanness through the lusts of their hearts, to dishonor their bodies between themselves: 25 Who changed the truth of God into a lie and worshiped and served the creature more than the Creator, who is blessed forever. Amen.

Even in the face of that lack of understanding on our part as Zimbabweans as we deified our leaders, God still wants to show us mercy. But we have to realize how far we have strayed from God through the choices that we have made over the years and then repent of all the iniquity and sin. I remember attending a political rally in the Midlands in which the master of ceremonies commented when a pastor had asked people to close their eyes and pray, "I was scared to close my eyes in prayer because that is how we lost our soil heritage." The statement sounded slick, but God hears and records our actions all the time. Inadvertently, the master of ceremonies may not have realized that he was accusing God of being a colonialist because worshiping God is an act that is separate from colonialism. Yes, the saying that the flag followed the cross is true, but God is not an author of greed. In any way, two wrongs do not make a right because by reacting to the pain of colonialism, we omitted humility and rebelled against God.

Instead of separating God from man's greed, our national leaders fell into the trap of Satan, and the nation was plunged into darkness. Marxism was not only embraced as an ideology. It became a religion. While the cause for the liberation of Zimbabwe was very noble, the ignoble thing that grafted itself into the cause was the refusal by the leaders to give God the glory for enabling them to stand up for what is right in challenging colonial oppression. God is the one who has the times and seasons of life in His hands and not Nehanda, Kaguvi, Mukwati, or any other fallen hero. The hero who did not fall is Jesus Christ, who defeated death, and He did all that to redeem us from sin. Jesus Christ has an issue with people who turn their backs on Him for any reason. As you can read from the verses in Romans Chapter One referenced above, they claimed that God's creation cared for them more than Himself, which is not true.

Chapter 17
Totems

Romans 1: 23 points out another critical belief and practice among Zimbabweans, which has been venerated for centuries. Such beliefs and practices do not become right because many people practice them. What God says about them is what matters. The verse says, *And changed the glory of the incorruptible God into an image made like to corruptible man, and to birds, and four-footed beasts, and creeping things.*

Our understanding of the word of God and its absolute power is very critical to any decisions that we make. The level of bondage that comes through totems is cause for concern to any right-thinking believer. If we apply Romans 1:23 to the Zimbabwean tradition, then the whole nation needs to repent from the sin of changing the glory of the incorruptible God into an image made like corruptible man, birds, and four-footed beasts and creeping things. Some of these sinful practices have become second nature to us, and we see nothing wrong with it, but God does.

We practice idolatry daily. When you hear Soko, people brag that they are a baboon or monkey- Mukanya, paying homage to spirits connected to that animal without even understanding the bondage that comes with such acts.

It could even be Soko/ Murehwa/ Mbire/Ncube; Dhuve/Duve/Dube- Mutasa, Manjenjenje, Chishongo chavasikana… People gloat over such Shona praise poetry, but behind it is complex patterns of behavior and attitudes that characterize people who belong to such totems, and they never explore why. The reason why they do not explore such matters is the complexity of the customs and hierarchical structures of relations and fear-mongering that weaken individuals from challenging such structures.

The animals, birds, body organs, and marine creatures our ancestors chose to be their totems were not an act of affection and attraction to a particular animal group. Theirs were relations created through covenants of blood, binding the descendants of such partakers of the covenant to be the progeny of the covenant animal. The type of covenants entered into by our ancestors to establish totems is not different from initiation into Freemasonry or any other cult or secret society. How do human beings take on animal characteristics and be happy about them? The animal characteristics come with rituals that initiate every generation into the family rites of passage from conception to adulthood. The practices are part of the traditional practices that are looked at as a way of doing things, and even believers in Christ Jesus land their support to such practices. If you challenge such practices, no one has a satisfactory answer except to say, "This is what we do in this family" These practices lock up an individual from birth to certain personality traits; physical features; attitudes, and behavior patterns that align with the spiritual governmental system that rules a tribe or family called Mhondoro. Does one wonder if we will ever know how some people would have lived or made choices about their destinies if such bondages did not exist? We know Nzou/Elephant, Shava/Mhofu, Nguruve/Ngulube, Hove/ Fish/Save, Shumba-Mhari, Shumba- Nyamuzihwa, Mlilo/Moto, Nyati/Nyathi.

The Mhondoro spirits rule all the provinces of Zimbabwe by permission granted to them many centuries ago, and every generation renews this control through different rituals that are done seasonally. The regional Mhondoro spirits answer to the national mhondoro at Matobo, at the Njelele shrine. These spirits have powers over rain and fertility, and if they are angered, they can disrupt the lives of their worshippers.
When you closely examine the characteristics of these ruling spirits, then, you realize that you are describing Baal or Ashteroth of Canaan. This is very strange, but looking at the drunken orgies during the chief's inauguration ceremony, you realize also that that is the way Ashteroth is worshiped. If the chief goes through rituals of honoring these spirits before he can rule, then the mhondoro spirits are in charge, and the chief is only a figurehead. That would also entail that anyone under the leadership of the chief is subject to those spirits, and even the land they live on belongs to spirits. That leaves the chief and his people as subjects of these higher powers. If any curses are operating in that particular area, then the chief and his people and the soil that they walk on are cursed. If the women are cursed with a

certain deformity, then the whole area succumbs to that problem. This is because a certain type of spirit with powers to cause certain ailments is in charge of the area with full rights. Only the blood of Jesus Christ can dislodge such a power.

These ruling powers work according to rank; principalities, powers, and strongholds hold some form of power and exert their influence on individuals and families. That is why some areas are renowned for witchcraft, others for prostitution, and yet others for bloodshed. This is dictated by the strongholds of the area, which rule through ancient covenants that give them the right to do so. For instance, the chief's symbolic act of having sex in the pool with his daughter or sister during his inauguration to the throne is worshipping mhondoro spirits. Why does the act have to be vile like that? It is because the act has to demonstrate all defiance against the laws of God to prove who is in control of the people of Zimbabwe. To those engaging in the act, it is a tradition, but spiritually, it is high-level sacrilege. If regional spirits of the waters honored at ceremonies are in charge of the regions, they also answer to the national spirit. In other words, the ruling spirit of Zimbabwe is in charge of the waters, the soil, and the people by right. Scholars concur that Zimbabweans worship a common ancestor, a marine spirit.

Aeneas Chigwedere, in his book from *Mutapa to Rhodes* (Macmillan, 1980), points out that the dynasties in Zimbabwe have a common ancestor hence common national religious guardian.

Jinda Mutinhima, a religious reporter, in his article in The Sunday Mail of January 24, 2016, titles *Nyakasikana, the unspoken mermaid spirit of Nzunza,* points out that Nyamita and Chaminuka were taken by mermaid spirits and due to that development, Nyamita was possessed by the spirit of Nehanda Nyakasikana. Chaminuka and Nyamita were the children of Murengasororenzou or Toho yaNdou in Venda.

Chaminuka is not as prominent as Nehanda, but he possessed rainmaking powers in his territory of long grass called Dungwiza or Chitungwiza.

Jinda Mutinhima points out that " The spirits of Chaminuka and Nehanda had a relation with water spirits" Legend supports the territorial spiritual power of Chaminuka in a song commonly sung in Zimbabwe;
Chaminuka ndimambo-o

A he he ndiMambo-o
A he he ndiMambo
Wakariga mukono we Manhize!
This one-stanza song corroborates Chaminuka's relationship with the marine world by pointing out that his rulership strength was demonstrated in his ability to topple a strongman of the pool called Manhize Chikapakapa in Mhondoro. In other words, Chaminuka did not only exercise authority over humans, but he had dormancy over the marine world of the area that he ruled. From this, we can deduce that political power alone is not enough to traditionally rule Zimbabwe. One has to be a stronghold in the spirit and the natural. Today, Chamunika is remembered as one of the veteran leaders of Zimbabwe. Historians are right that the nation is ruled by a common ancestor, a mermaid. However, they do not elaborate on how such leadership expresses itself on the ground, as well as its impact on the day-to-day lives of people. While such a territory can claim to belong to God/god, serious questions have to be asked as to which God/god is worshiped since the God of heaven does not share His glory with any of His creations.

Jinda Mutinhima also points out in his article that there was another Nyakasikana, a mermaid spirit that resides in the Nzunza mountain in Nyanga. Her other name is Semukadzi which is consulted through the Simboti totem. Nyakasikana of Nzunza has fertility powers, and although she lives in the Nzunza mountains, she patrols other sacred rivers in the eastern highlands.

On the other hand, sacred rivers like Save are the totem of the Musikavanhu/Mlambo/ Hove people of the Fish totem. It means that when they invoke the family or tribal spirits of the Save people, they connect with or worship the ruling spirit called Semukadzi/ Nyakasikana. This mermaid has rain-making powers and is believed to lead to abundant harvests in Manicaland.

Interestingly, Semukadzi or Nyakasikana prevented bad omens from the seas into Manicaland. In other words, Semukadzi prevents the activities of Neptune or Poseidon, the god of the Oceans and king of the rivers, storms, floods, drought, earthquakes, and horses, from proceeding further mainland into Zimbabwe. Cyclone Idai seems to have defied the powers of Semukadzi if such a ruling spirit exists in the region.

The role of Semukadzi can be equated to that of Nyaminyami (A snake like a mermaid) in the Zambezi Valley.

Jinda Mutinhima says, "This belief of worshiping marine spirits through ancestors is not peculiar to Zimbabwe alone but the world over. For example, in Congo near Lubumbashi, the people have their version of Nyakasikana, and the medium is called Nakamwale, meaning adolescent girl, which is the same as Nyakasikana.

According to Jinda Mutinhima, the worship of marine spirits is done worldwide. In other words, it is a system that is pervasive. So, when we say we are going back to our tradition, we are just proclaiming that we are walking away from the ways of God because what we call tradition is not unique to us but a global practice. Only that we have a pattern of fitting into that system different from Europeans and Asians, but we are all doing the same thing. What is that same thing? We worship the god of this world through a cunningly devised system that makes us believe that what we are doing is unique to us only. Yet, it is not so. In so doing, we express that we have perfected the system of worshiping the ruler of the darkness of this world to whom we are paying obeisance.

God is saying, "Repent from all the deception" and turn to Him, who is the source of all things, even the happiness and wealth that we desperately look for.

Chapter 18
The Ruling spirits of Zimbabwe

Murenga- the ruling spirit at Matobo at Njelele
Characteristics

Murenga or Mulimo is the ruling spirit of Zimbabwe which speaks from its shrine in Matobo. This writer is trying to understand why the dwelling place of Murenga is called a shrine and not an altar. The spirit of Murenga is a warrior spirit, and as many Zimbabwean historians have pointed out, wars are fought in the name of Murenga. The two wars called the First Chimurenga or Chindunduma and the Second Chimurenga, are believed to have been fought under the spiritual command of the national spirit. Murenga has children, who are Nehanda and Chaminuka, who are responsible for organizing wars. Although we pray for peace in our country, it appears to be a waste of time because we made a covenant or we are being ruled by a spirit characterized by bloodshed. Do you realize why road/motor vehicle accidents never cease every public holiday taking so many lives on our roads? It is because we have agreed that the Murenga spirit is the ruler of Zimbabwe, but this spirit is a spirit of conflict, it is bloody, and it is a spirit of the husband which partly contributes to the carnage on the roads. Murenga is also a water spirit or mermaid. This explains why some chiefs at the grassroots have sex with family members in a pool or river because the local leader has to pay homage to the national spirit through such a ritual. The new ruler/ chief has to salute the actual ruler upon his inauguration by engaging in incest, Whether the chief likes it or not, he has to go through this rite. The chief's views on incest do not matter because tradition requires him to do so. All the practices from the family unit to the national level are an organized hierarchy of marine worship.

Besides incest in the pool or river, chiefs also go to the same places locally for rain-making ceremonies because Murenga is a deity of fertility and rain. Barren women go to Njelele to ask for children, and many barren women manage to conceive. Their conception proves the fertility powers of the deity. That practice begs many questions because the one who creates people is God Almighty. So, where does the Baal/Murenga deity derive the powers to make people conceive? The Bible points out that even Satan disguises himself as an angel of light. Lying wonders are mentioned in the bible, and the ability to make people conceive is one of them. Remember Genesis 6. The sons of God went in/ had sexual relations with the daughters of men, and a human race called the Nephilim was born. It is important to know that this race of people did not have the DNA of God, and they cannot serve God, nor can they repent. This group was resident in Canaan during the arrival of the children of Israel. These are a race of people who were men of renown. In other words, we begin to hear of celebrity status from this race of people. They were great achievers, and their physique scared the people of Israel- *"We saw the Nephilim there (the descendants of Anak come from the Nephilim). We seemed like grasshoppers in our own eyes, and we looked the same to them.* "Numbers 13:33. This is a seed of beings which thrives among us today, and as we worship blindly, without searching diligently, what it is that we worship, through subtlety, we are drawn into a worship of the Nephilim.

That dastardly worship causes us to lose our heritage in God. God tells Israel not to mix with that race because they would contaminate the human race. This is not a talk about some races being superior to others, like the claims of the Aryan race under Hitler, but a satanic move designed to contaminate humanity so that salvation becomes impossible, resulting in an eternity in hell. The race of the Nephilim cannot be saved because, like Satan, they were not born through the law of God, of the relationship between man and woman, resulting in conception, pregnancy, and birth.

Mbonga

From time to time, the spirit of Njelele sends virgin girls from different parts of the country who are brought to the shrine to be the wives of Njelele. The women stay at the shrine at Matobo. How does a spirit marry human beings? This brings us back to Genesis 6:2, where sons of God - angels who are spirits, are said to have married the daughters of men. In other words, what Mlimo does, is a very ancient act of rebellion against God, but our nation venerates that spirit as the national ruler. These girls are called Mbonga. They are the wives of an unseen being. Their families do not dispute the orders from Njelele. They send a daughter who will never return to the family until she dies. She stays at the shrine all the days of her life. This act of having women marry a spirit is the foundation of the bondage of many by what is called spirit husbands or spirit wives in Zimbabwe.

The spirit husband/ wife
In the bible, Genesis 6:4, and also in the Book of Enoch, the forbidden sexual encounters between human beings and angelic beings, which are spirits, took place, and giants were born to them like Goliath of Gath, and his brothers, Og, king of Bashan, and Sihon, king of the Amorites. Is it possible that the whole nation of Zimbabwe worships a national spirit from the family of the giants mentioned in the Bible? Part of this history has been mentioned earlier. The effect of humans marrying spirits needs to be examined in terms of the impact on the livelihood of individuals, marriage, and lifestyle choices. Some legends talk about the

incubus and succubus spirits which are believed to be male and female spirits that attack individuals sexually in their sleep. Although this is presented as a remote belief, this is a stronghold in Zimbabwe that is responsible for ravaging marriages and human lives. We call them marine spirits or spirit husbands, or spirit wives. They have their hierarchy from Njelele, trickling down to the regions where they are given access through covenantal rituals or totems to access women or men sexually. When a chief engages in drunken orgies, he does not stop after the occasion because the spirit behind the orgies and incest gains access to a person's life when the rituals are done. Such rituals, like *kupira mudzimu-traditional ceremonies to appease the dead,* are called door openers because the rituals are acts of worship and give the spirits unfettered control over households and individuals. These same patterns are also employed in killing individuals in families from a spiritual point of view.

A spirit husband claims a girl or woman as his wife once it has been given access through rituals. The spirit presents itself to its victim through dreams, or some women or men see dark shadows entering their bedrooms and onto their beds. They freeze with fear and pass out and only wake up knowing that they have had a sexual encounter. Sometimes they feel dirty because something inordinate has been deposited in their spirit. When such encounters persist, the behavior of the woman who is a victim of an involuntary sexual encounter can change drastically. They develop fear at night because of the attacks in the night by a spirit husband or spirit wife. Some women develop gynecological complications that can be fatal. Rituals that attract spirit husbands or wives are not done by chiefs only. Families in search of wealth and influence are drawn by greed into opening doors to these spirits, and their children become victims.

Sometimes, spirit husbands are introduced into the family through ritual murders. In the past, the practice of **kutema ugariri** – *was in which a man would work for years for a family with the understanding that after several stipulated years, the family would give him one of their daughters to marry.* That is the story of Jacob in Genesis 29 in the Bible, who worked for his father-in-law, herding cattle and other animals for years to get a wife. He ended up with two. In the early years of colonial settlement in southern Africa, there was a lot of internal migration in search of employment. Citizens of other countries passed through Zimbabwe searching for employment in the South African mines. Some of the migrants ended up working for Zimbabwean families. The hired foreigners were promised payment for their wages with one of the family's daughters. This is what Jacob of the Bible did. He worked for Laban of Syria for seven years for a wife.

For many migrant domestic workers, when the time came for the man to be given a wife, most families broke that agreement. They refused to give the wife to their laborer, and some went to the extent of killing their former employee as a way of silencing or using him for ritual purposes. Some women from such families struggle to keep marriages because there is an unresolved broken agreement with a man who was not paid his wages by previous generations. When people break covenants or even kill an innocent person, they open their bloodline to the avenger of blood as mentioned in the bible or in Shona, it is called **Ngozi.** This is primitive spiritual justice that curses a whole bloodline, especially women. It can only succumb to the blood of Jesus Christ. So, when people use the traditional route, they do not solve the problem because this type of spirit claims to have legal rights over the girls of a particular bloodline which is a legal claim in the spirit which can only be atoned for by the blood of Jesus Christ. When people understand why Jesus died on the cross, they also have an understanding that he paid the price for them so that they can be free. Sometimes, even after becoming Christians, the Holy Spirit can instruct some members of some families to pay reparations for the crimes of their fathers. Every case is different, but the Holy Spirit knows the truth of every case and can help those who have the humility to seek peace and resolution of any existing conflict.

Women married to spirit husbands bear spiritual children who live under the waters. It is like a person lives in two worlds; one unseen and the other visible. This is a spiritual dynamic. A human being can live on earth but have a thriving relationship with spirits that live underwater to the extent of marrying them and bearing children, a woman who looks ordinary in everyday life can be a queen under the waters, and her spirit husband would be king. In such cases, if some women insist on marrying an earthly husband without deliverance, the spirit husband can kill the human husband. The spirit of the avenger can do the same thing too. That is why some

Pentecostal churches of old recommended marrying after hearing God. Even seeking prayers before attaching to a partner is necessary because an innocent life may be endangered.

Chapter 19
Troubled Marriages

Marriages influenced by negative spiritual influences suffer from a lack of happiness and intimacy and supplant the possibility of a conducive environment for a healthy upbringing of children. The Zimbabwean woman is renowned for her strength and ability to withstand adversity throughout her life, in marriage, at work, and in raising her children. This is not something we imagine but a reality that many of us know very well. Very often, this suffering is an accepted norm. What has been ignored is finding out why the woman's life is in such a condition. In exploring the underlying problems of marriages in Zimbabwe, based on the numbers of women and men who seek deliverance, it is clear in most cases that cultural beliefs and practices are at the center of some of the problems. The lack of understanding of what is being worshiped and how it impacts the individual in society leaves many individuals without the capacity to gain freedom from what they experience. This destructive power of the spirits we worship is mostly at the root of domestic violence in Zimbabwe. This often comes out in spiritual deliverance sessions, where the spirits identify themselves and their mission in an individual's life. The spirits fight to remain in the person's life because they say- *"Takamupiwa. Ndewedu"*- *"This person was given to us. This person belongs to us"* The host of such spirits becomes a slave to them. The person does the bidding of the host demons. Sometimes, the demons abuse, harass, confuse, and even kill the person. With such oppression, it is easy for the victim to be unkind to the person next to the victim, who can be a child or wife/husband. Have you ever wondered why some men never stop beating on their wives or even murdering them? This is because, in cases of demonic bondage to marine spirits, a man or woman marries an individual who is already in a marriage relationship with a spirit without knowing it because the other husband or wife is invisible.

    In marriage counseling, those of us of Zimbabwean descent have a checklist when a marriage is troubled. We seek to understand if there are marine spirits involved or just general demonic possession. Marine spirits commonly use verbal abuse. Since they are not visible, they use the wife or the husband to say words that hurt the partner. The level of hurt is akin to emotional paralysis because the words are not ordinary. They are released with a demonic influence that hurts the hearer to seriously consider a divorce. Divorce is what marine spirits want because they are jealous partners who are unseen. It is common for marine spirits to enter their victim through an act of rape, incest, molestation, and sodomy. After such an act, the victim's emotions are paralyzed to no recovery for many. These women struggle with decision-making because their emotions do not develop at the pace of their normal bodily development. Consequently, they exhibit a maturity of age mingled with infantile episodes that confuse their partners. Deliverance of emotional paralysis can bring about an emotional balance in the victim.

The first test is whether the couple fights over words. What happens is that when there is a spirit husband in a relationship, the wife may say an innocent statement to her husband. "Why don't you put on the blue shirt because the burgundy one does not match that pair of trousers?" What the husband may hear can be something like this, "Look at you; you cannot even dress up properly without me helping you out. Look at you!" The husband then says in response, "What have you just said? My mother taught me how to dress well. Please stop trying to control me" The wife then says, "What are you talking about? I just said that that pair of trousers does not match that shirt only. How does your mother come into the equation?" The husband then says, "I am not deaf. I heard you. And please do not despise my mother. She did a good job" From that conversation, the couple won't speak to each other for a whole week. That is a sign of the presence of a spirit, usually of marine origin. The spirit twists the words between the love birds to foment trouble. The reason why the spirit does this is that very often, when couples are fighting, they also deny each other conjugal rights. However, that does not mean that both of them will be going without sex because the one with the marine partner will have exclusive sex without the interference of the human partner. The longer the couple takes without communicating, the better the chance of the marine spirit to have sex with the other partner without sharing. This is one of the consequences produced by the spirits that we bow down to as a nation or family.

The second test is whether one of the spouses ever has dreams of having sex with a stranger. If that is confirmed, you know that there is a third party in marriage called a spirit husband or spirit wife. Sometimes, husbands complain that their wives deny them their conjugal rights, but at night, the husband hears his wife actively involved in a sexual encounter with a man that the husband cannot see. When the husband asks for intimacy, the wife usually says she is always tired. This can be done by the husband if he is the one with a marine spirit wife. One woman once pointed out, "All I do is survive on masturbation because my husband has sex with an unseen woman. I change wet bed sheets daily because of his sexual encounters with an unseen partner."

The third checklist is whether any one of the spouses ever has dreams of swimming. This is a sign that one of them has trips under the waters, either for witchcraft purposes or as a spirit husband or wife visit in the marine kingdom.

The process of deliverance can be complicated because some women or men have amassed power in their connection with the marine spirits. They get to a point where they have morphed into half-human beings and half-mermaids. Such spouses appear in that form to their husbands or wives at night because that spirit works in conjunction with witchcraft.

The fourth checklist during deliverance in marriages is that a spouse may also notice the existence of both male and female sexual organs on the wife- the androgynous quality of Ashtoreth. This explains why some of the people possessed by such spirits do not have the desire to marry. They are androgynous like Ashteroth, the Canaanite deity, which is also the stronghold with such features. They can satisfy themselves sexually because they are a full package, both male and female. There is no need for an outsider in the form of a wife or husband. In case there happens to be a husband to a wife with such a form of existence, that spirit emasculates him so that the wife is the one with the authority of a husband in the home. This is not necessarily a fact that the wife rules the roost, but the spirit husband attacks the natural husband through her. These spirits can kill the husband through accidents, strangulation, or beating him down until he submits to the wife. Many homes are in a predicament where the wife rules the husband with disdain because the husband is a slave responsible for bringing in money. Other resources so that the spirit husband and the woman can enjoy. Most of the unfortunate experiences in marriages in Zimbabwe are caused mainly by the national worship system. On the other hand, when a family has altars of bloodshed, you may notice patterns that the first child born in any marriage in the family dies through miscarriage, and then the ones that follow would be fine. The reason why the first child dies is that the new marriage would be paying or contributing to the blood banks of the family with their unborn child. If that does not happen, then the marriage may not subsist because it has not met the requirements of the family altars. This is called sacrificing at the altar of Molech. Molech was a Canaanite god whom the ancient people worshiped by boiling children alive.

The fifth checklist is that of relations between spouses. The most common problem in marriages is infidelity. Very often, women from families that have wealth, are in commercial farming, or some business can find themselves engaging in adultery, but their husbands would not divorce them. The spirit of orgies can become a part of a family's altars, where all the daughters have to engage in sexual immorality, especially infidelity, as a way of servicing family altars. Most of the time, such women are divorced and end up having many sexual partners, and that is exactly what is written in the codes or ordinances of their family altars. If they do not conform to that pattern, the wife or husband may die. In some cases, children with disabilities are born, but not always.

The spirit husband/ wife cluster of spirits that rule Zimbabwe is very dangerous, and venerating them is courting trouble for the nation.

They can desensitize their victim from a young age by exposing them to sexualized environments and sometimes through rape/sodomy and sexually explicit materials like pornography. The child then assumes nothing is wrong with a particular lifestyle because demons have worked on innocent emotions, arousing them to a place where sexual pleasure becomes a part of their lives at an early age. They sexually act out as teenagers because they do not understand that their behavior is wrong. After all, it is a practice introduced to them as part and parcel of life.

The sixth checklist is **incest**- it is not surprising that incestuous relations are a gateway to initiating daughters or sons into sexual relations at an early age. This is done as a ritual in many cases. It is an act of worship of the ruling spirits of the family line. The children are psychologically damaged and, in many cases, have no recourse because the perpetrators are authoritative figures in the family. This experience is common among orphans, stepchildren, and children from some well-to-do families. These are vulnerable members of a family who may have nowhere to report by their circumstances. Unfortunately, victimization alters their moods and behaviors. Very often, the violent nature of the initial sexual encounter opens the victim to possession by evil spirits of the marine type because God designed a woman to lose her virginity on the night of her wedding.

However, the violation is not only a desecration of an innocent person's body; it is also a violation of the law of God relating to chastity. Many rapes, molestation, incestuous, and sodomy cases have a spiritual origin and influence to open up the person to a dwelling place of spirits. The spirits can be different, like promiscuity, stealing, lack of impulse control, anxiety, and fear. The violation of the child becomes like a garden that has been broken into. Thereby enabling other illegal entries/violations by both humans and spirits. This is usually the entry point of homosexual spirits, spirit wives, and husbands. Watching pornography also opens people within the environment to perversion. A pregnant woman who watches pornography can expose her unborn child to a perverse sexual orientation. I remember a woman who enjoyed watching pornography with her boyfriend, and the child that she bore got addicted to pornography by the age of seven. The child had no idea of the lifestyle of her mother before she was born, but she struggled to ward off pornography addiction. Pornography is an inhuman sexual encounter where two people. a human being and an animal have sexual encounters under the influence of drugs. The women are, in many cases, victims of human sex trafficking who are not engaging in sex for pleasure but are enslaved by pimps or drug lords. The drugs that are administered to pornography partners are from drug trafficking rings. The drug traffickers offer the drugs to deities, asking them to influence the drugs to be intoxicating to the people who take them. The sex slaves are forced to take these drugs. The whole act is a gross violation of the human rights of other people to give pleasure to people in foreign lands who have no idea that by watching these pornographic scenes, they are opening their lives to heavy demonic bondage. They also have no idea that once such a door is opened, their offspring is sucked into perversion. Many parents of today owe their children apologies for causing untold suffering to innocent members of the family through addiction to pornography.

Some wayward behavior exhibited by children may have a direct connection with the parents' lifestyle before they marry or even during the marriage. Some divorces are directly linked to pornographic practices because once a person is addicted to watching beastly sexual behavior, no fun is derived from sex with another human being of the opposite sex. This has come from the confessions of individuals during deliverance. Some people then turn to masturbation or even Sado masochism for satisfaction. Sado-Masochism is a psychosexual disorder in which sexual gratification is obtained by engaging in sadistic and masochistic interactions.

Unfortunately, spirit husbands/wives come from a group of marine spirits-Nephilim which then forbid their host from having natural emotional attachments to another human being because they are jealous, just like any spouse. They can kill the other spouse, as said before, cause divorce, or cause unmanageable havoc in the marriage. Not every woman or man possessed by these spirits seeks deliverance. Some people are comfortable with having sex with a spirit. They know it, and they are fine with it too. This is because spirits come with allurements of power. This is more common among adults who choose to acquire wealth at any cost, in which the end justifies the means, than in children who are mostly products of victimization.

They can also bring wealth to the person who invited them, but in exchange for the wealth, they ask for a human host from among the relatives of the person who invited them. This is why some young children are sacrificed to these spirits by their parents through other methods. Incest, in particular, is part of the ritual. Some family members sacrifice their young relatives in such lives, all for the sake of gain. Remember, these acts cease to be just commissions of crimes, but it is a way of worshiping that is part of the culture, evil as it may sound.

How to know if you have such problems
Involvement in sexual sins. Not every prostitute enjoys what she does, and not every male adulterer does. The concept of 'small house' has these demonic roots. Many people are unaware that one sure way to cut off your life expectancy is through sexual immorality. While people cry out about the poverty in Zimbabwe, and the reduced years of life, sexual behavior also adds to the dilemma. Before God, a person who engages in sexual sin defies the concept of one man and woman. This defiance has a spiritual significance, too, because it despises the earthly representation of a divine plan called marriage. Proverbs is full of warnings and instructions about the behavior of young men. It is totally against the sowing of one's oats. As a young man sows his oats, he is also contaminating the seed that he carries. -Sex in the dreams is a sexual encounter with a spirit, warlock, and or a witch.
-Seeing yourself by the river in your dreams.
-Love for ornaments or jewelry made of or shaped like creatures from the sea. One time, a beloved friend gave my family some seashell jewelry. An elder standing by then said, "Let us

test the authenticity of the shells because if they are genuine, you can hear the sound of the waves of the sea" In other words, some items from the great deep carry the stamp of their origin wherever they go. How many people consider such matters when they buy different kinds of jewelry?
-Love for images and pictures that relate to or are from under the sea.

What does the word of God say about the forgiveness of iniquity?

Yes, God gives us the room to acknowledge our iniquities as a condition for their purging. In other words, iniquity is behind most of the bondages that believers suffer from, but God can forgive the iniquity of that sin, thereby rendering the sin lifeless.

Psalm 32: 5
I acknowledge my sin unto thee, and mine iniquity have I not hid. I said I will confess my transgressions unto the LORD, and thou forgavest the iniquity of my sin. Selah.

Psalm 65: 3

*Iniquities prevail against me, but as for our transgressions, you shall purge
them away.*

Isaiah 49: 24-25
Shall the prey be taken from the mighty, or the lawful captive be delivered?
*But thus the Lord, Even the captives of the mighty shall be taken away, and the prey of the terrible shall be delivered: for I will contend with him
that contendeth with thee, and I will save thy children.*

Covenants with marine spirits
Syncretism

Some Zimbabweans make covenants with Murenga and all his spirits that rule the regions when our chiefs hold rain-making ceremonies where they evoke the marine spirits. The Rozvi/ Destroyers are at the helm of this practice as the acclaimed founders of Zimbabwe.

The danger comes when people who have confessed Jesus as their Lord and Savior move on to engage in the same style of worship by identifying with their tribal totems because at the helm of the tribal line are marine spirits. This means that by boasting about being a

Rozvi, you are saying. "I worship marine spirits" because, as a leading tribe, the Rozvi, at the helm of their power, presided over rain-making rituals at the national level. This is where idolatry comes in through iniquity. Whether through ignorance or presumption, whenever we claim to be Christians but have this inordinate relationship with our ancestors through totem chants, we contradict ourselves. Jesus says, *"Depart from me you workers of iniquity, I never knew you"*- Matthew 7:21. Syncretism is a union or attempted fusion of different religions, cultures, or philosophies. Many professing Christians will be shocked on the Day of Judgment because their strongly held traditional beliefs weakened their walk with God, resulting in a disqualification from eternity.

To show you that the spirit realm is different from our natural realm, it is Zimbabwean historians and sociologists who have made an issue about Cecil John Rhodes's grave being at Matobo. Did you ever hear the voice at the Njelele shrine give orders for Rhodes's grave to be removed? Why not? It is because it is the same kingdom whether the messenger is white or black, the mission of keeping people in perpetual bondage is achieved. Njelele has a mouth and can cleanse Matopo by giving orders to do away with Rhodes' grave. We have a problem as people in general because we identify darkness with race or gender, but darkness is darkness; it is a spiritual phenomenon. Let us wake up and not be hoodwinked by demonic fads of racial prejudice because we have shed innocent blood behind these differences.

Chapter 20

The Flag of Zimbabwe

The flag of Zimbabwe has five different colors; green, red, black and white. Then a golden bird called the African Fish Eagle. Behind the bird is a red star which some say symbolizes socialism which the ruling party ZANU pf which designed the flag was affiliated with.

The green on the flag represents agriculture. Red represents bloodshed in the First and Second Chimurenga. Black symbolizes the heritage of black people. White represents peace and, maybe to a certain extent, the white population that is part and parcel of the nation's history. The Golden Bird or African Fish Eagle represents the strong bond that ancestral humans had with animals, nature, and spiritual guides. The bird is perched on a chair that can be taken to represent the authority of the ancient Great Zimbabwe throne.

The presence of the red star on the flag is not elaborated on as the other colors. There has been deliberate glossing over whenever the flag's colors are explained, with the emphasis being on the major colors and the red being treated exactly in the manner in which it is situated, behind the bird. The red star has five points representing a pentagram There is no known Shona or Ndebele tradition associated with the pentagram. The number 5 is associated with the planet Mars, the Roman god of war and bloodshed. It signifies severity, conflict, and harmony through conflict. Remember the ZANU pf mantra during the liberation struggle broadcasting from Mozambique, *winning through the gun barrel,* thereby bringing peace through conflict. Mars was associated with fever, accidents, trauma, pain, and hunger. Admittedly, some decisions were made out of the pain of oppression. Yet, God remains sovereign and wants us to be true to our commitment to reconciliation, uniting the country in fear and reverence of His Name. The pentagram has a Martian connection which is bloody. When national symbols connect to dubious practices and beliefs, it becomes difficult to know whether the intention was to continuously shed blood or it was a seduction into bondage during the liberation struggle for our leaders. This is because secretive organizations like freemasonry played a significant role in the fall of empires and decolonization, beginning with Spain. No one has ever asked what that pentagram-shaped red star means on the Zimbabwean flag. According to Merriam-Webster Dictionary, a pentagram is a figure of a 5-pointed star usually made with alternate points connected by a continuous line and used as a magic or occult symbol.

The Zimbabwe bird also is the fish eagle which is connected to the marine world. In other words, national symbols point to the nature of national worship strongly connected to water bodies.

Chapter 21
Kurapira/ protection rituals

Each family has certain types of rituals done to a child at birth. Some rituals are very simple, like applying ashes on the fontanel. Yet when one digs deeper into the significance of such a simple act through prayer, one understands that the ashes put on the head of an innocent baby were symbolic. The baby is offered to strange gods of fire. That child may never prosper in their life, and if they do, the gods who claim the child's destiny consume like fire all the fruit of the child's labor. These strange gods can consume marriage, and then you see a marriage crumble without a plausible explanation. Yet the reason behind such fate is seemingly harmless ashes applied to the child in the formative years. It takes the grace of God for such people to hold wealth, marriage, and success for long periods. It is no surprise that in Zimbabwe, there is hardly any legacy of wealth generation because of the scattering spirits that children are offered at birth, and no one escapes that passage one way or another. The Bible says in Isaiah 61:3 that *God gives us beauty for ashes*. How do we get it twisted by wishing a newborn well by applying ashes? It is my opinion that the process of applying ashes limits a person's ability to reach their maximum potential in life. It is like a ceiling over what an individual can do and become. That may explain the short life expectancy in some families too. However, in Zimbabwe, idolatry has impacted life expectancy too, because of disease, famine, and a difficult environment for a comfortable existence.

When we offer our children at birth to familial spirits through **mishonga yamasuwo (Concoctions that aid the pregnancy and birthing process), kurapira nhova- rites of the fontanel, we are practicing idolatry, and we surrender the protection of that child to powers of darkness.** God cannot challenge our choices because we have free will. That does not change the fact that we are responsible for the bondage that the newborn experiences later in life. Jesus was clear about His relationship to children in Matthew 19:14, But Jesus said," *Suffer little children, and forbid them not, to come unto me: for of such is the kingdom of heaven.*" Again in Matthew 18: 10, Jesus Christ says, *"Take heed that ye despise not one of these little ones; for I say unto you, That in heaven their angels do always behold the face of my Father which is in heaven"*

Have you ever heard the Shona people say, *"Nhova yeChiNdevere yakasimba, inotunga dzimwe"- The fontanel ritual of the Ndebele is strong and subdues the Shona one.* If the process yenhova- *fontanel rite* is just a harmless ritual, how do the elders talk of spiritual tribal confrontation at that infancy level when children who do not yet know much about the world around them are subjected to familial rituals? There are many cases where people say that a child is not ill, but her protection has been overridden by more powerful protection from another baby. In other words, by applying some concoctions on a baby's fontanel, the ritual enables a living spirit to enter the child. Whether the spirit is weak or strong, there is something that the child carries after that ritual. The sad thing is that the mother, who is usually very young at that stage or is full of fear, has no idea of what the child has been subjected to. She is bullied into accepting lasting changes in her child without a clue of the effect of the ritual on the child.

Chapter 22
Rape Victims

There have been many cases of rape in Zimbabwe, and perpetrators do not stop committing the crime in spite of heavy sentences that such crimes carry. The court system clashes with tradition in terms of the classification of rape. The court defines rape as a punishable crime, but Shona tradition propounds something else. Sexual performance is not just an act among Shona men or other cultures. It is a sign of virility and strength. The strength cannot be defined as such until its potency is proven. The pressure to prove their manhood is real among many young men. Whatever they do to prove it is encouraged in many subtle ways from their childhood, while the girls are warned to keep their virginity until their wedding night. That tilts the scales of freedom in favor of the male child and often gives them a license to think that proving their manhood supersedes respect for boundaries with the opposite sex.

This strength is exploited by customary belief systems that are spiritual. This is especially so when family covenants or altars of power also include sexual rituals. The man in families with covenants with marines' spirits, in particular, often have sex for more than just pleasure. It is used by the kingdom of darkness to exploit youthful strength through ritual sex. Ritual sex is sex that is done as a form of worship and not pleasure, and this includes rape. In that manner, the whole act is a form of worship, and there is a spirit that drives them to do it. Since manhood is so prized, young men do not understand that they are being used to defile their bodies because God expressly says in His word that one thing that men will do before the throne of judgment is to give an account of how they spent their youth. Youthfulness is the peak of a man's strength. Ecclesiastes 11 says: 9 *"Rejoice, O young man, in thy youth, and let thy heart cheer thee in the days of thy youth, and walk in the ways of thine heart, and in the sight of thine eyes; but know thou, that for all these things God will bring thee to judgment"*

Unfortunately, our cultural practices set us at loggerheads with the law of God. When you read Ephesians 6, part of the spiritual armor that believers should wear includes verse 14, which says, *"Stand therefore, having your loins girt about with truth…."* The integrity of a man is in his loins because that is where he carries the seed of his bloodline. God intends to have that part of the body covered with the truth. If that integrity is violated in a young man's youth, when he finally decides to settle down, Satan fights his integrity. Remember, the Bible was originally written for men. Many people have devalued purity before and after marriage because a system contrary to the word of God influenced their upbringing. However, this does not absolve them from the consequences of disobedience to the word of God.

In Genesis 46: 26- *All the souls that came with Jacob into Egypt, which came out of his loins, besides Jacob's wives, all the souls were threescore and six.* Satan knows that if he can contaminate the integrity of a man through loose loins, then he gains control of the man's destiny, as well as that of his seed after him. Satan can claim lordship over a man's household once he has gained a foothold through sex outside marriage. What we may view as pleasure may be our entrance into the belly of hell without any chance of coming out. The Bible says in Proverbs 2 that a man must have wisdom, understanding, and discretion. These are given as safeguards against people who enjoy committing crimes and leave the paths of God. It also says the virtues of wisdom, knowledge, and discretion that deliver a young man from a strange woman, *even from the stranger flattered by her lips. Which forsaketh the guide of her youth, and forgetteth the covenant of her God. For her house inclineth unto death, and her paths unto the dead, None that go unto her return again, neither take they hold of the paths of life* (Proverbs 2:16-19). Proverbs 5: 1-5 " *My son, attend unto wisdom, and bow thine ear to my understanding. That thou mayest regard discretion and that thy lips may keep knowledge. For the lips of a strange woman drip like a honeycomb, and her mouth is smoother than oil. But her end is bitter as wormwood, sharp as a two-edged sword. Her feet go down to death, her steps take hold of hell.*" The verses mentioned above are God's warning to a young man on the secret of living longer, as well as cooperating with God regarding their wellbeing.

While some maids and babysitters molest the children under their care, the majority of sexual abuse is done by males, whether in the home or outside the home. The contamination of loins can span generations, and with each succeeding generation, careless sexual behavior becomes a common characteristic of iniquity. It is in the fray of iniquity that violating women can be regarded as a game. However, God frowns at such practices because they violate His laws. Some perpetrators of rape are never caught but their victims get a lifelong wound. Their lives are ravaged completely. Their pain, anger, and anguish of soul is a prayer of protest before God saying "God, when will I get justice for what was done to me? I did not choose this condition, someone used force on me to determine my future and destiny." When a victim cries before God, then God will not keep quiet. He will arise on behalf of the weak and fight for them in a just manner. Perpetrators pay for their crimes in one way or another unless they repent and ask God for forgiveness.

Careless sexual behavior opens doors to demonic attacks and oppression. These attacks result in demonic influence on personalities and their tastes, and direction in life can be hijacked by powers of darkness. There are patterns in families which indicate bondages that current generations struggle with, but they have no clue of where they came from.

Rape is also used to initiate young girls or children into prostitution for ritual purposes. A girl child rarely has the vision to grow up and become a prostitute. In families covenanted with the kingdom of darkness for purposes of fame, abundant harvests, and business success, girl children in some such families are sexually abused at a young age, but the act of violation will be demonically orchestrated. The girls do not choose a life of prostitution, but their defense mechanisms of the mind are distorted by the act of rape because of the age at which they are introduced to sex. They develop a mindset of understanding sex as an expression of love because they are confused about the purpose of sex. A young lady confided in me that when her uncle raped her from the age of five, she thought that sex was a normal part of life, and she began to teach her little brother, but when her mother saw her daughter training her son about sex, she did not investigate the matter. She thoroughly beat up the girl to stop her from continuing the behavior. Yet, the person who had molested her was living in the house and abused her daily without the mother's knowledge. The girl confessed that she had trouble forgiving her mother for not protecting her.

Have you ever observed a pattern in which family members rise and fall without any reasonable explanation? In some families, some disabilities rock every generation. Worse still, miscarriages can punctuate the beginning of a family. All these dark areas need to be dealt with and understood because there is a broader spiritual influence behind most of them.

Both perpetrators and victims in the case of rape, molestation, and incest need deliverance.

Some effects of Rape on survivors.

Sex outside marriage is a door opener to bondage because God said that sex before marriage is a sin. For the chaste virgins, rape opens them up to further spiritual violations by evil spirits.

Self-mutilation. Survivors of rape cut themselves as a way of crying for help because they are going through so much turmoil in their minds, such that cutting oneself is viewed as a relief by the victim. The challenge that can alter the character of a survivor happens in the formative years because the victim may not understand the gravity of what happened to them. Still, the behavior that they exhibit would have been shaped by the violation that they would have undergone.

Regression. I regressed after rape back to a toddler. I could not recover for two years since I regressed from five to about two years old. Throughout life, I have always been behind my agemates by two years, whether in school or birth records, as well as graduation. Everything experienced a reversal of some kind in my life because I had to recover and move on. I was like a little girl who was once told she was a princess, and then someone overturned her little throne, and she found that she was somebody else who was unworthy of life.

Reinforcement of pre-existing issues. Rape reinforced rejection in my life.

Fear. I was afraid for many years and kept to myself out of fear of people. I would be aggressive in my responses so that people would leave me alone.

Speech impairment. I struggled to express myself for many years, making me a shy person because even my speech suffered some impairment because I was no longer sure of myself. I tended to run away if people made me angry because there was no point in talking to people who did not care about what I was going through.

Fantasy. I would fantasize about the day that I would be with my father and be happy again, but that never really happened for years. I waited for the day he would rescue me from what I was going through. Later in life, I realized that I was better off where I was no matter how hard life was for me. Fantasy is common among rape victims because some of them have out-of-body experiences, as they try to avoid the pain of sexual encounters at a tender age. I believe that I passed out during each rape episode because the intimidation alone was good enough to paralyze me. I only remember when the big boy threatened me before getting hold of my body. After that, I do not know what happened, but I would wake up with wet underwear. I had an out-of-body experience to flee from fear and the pain of sexual penetration. However, fantasy and out-of-body experiences make the victim access the spirit realm illegally, so they interact with spirits in that state. Through fantasy, some rape victims open up to **demonic spirit guides,** which are spirits that come into the life of a survivor early, purporting to comfort them in their pain, but these spirits never leave because they would have found a body to dwell in. They begin to shape the child's character in the direction of destruction. They influence emotions, tastes, attitudes, and a negative view of life. Demonic spirit guides confuse the individual in the process of growth and development. They have a special interest in confusing the decision-making process because of their inability to focus. Some survivors of rape do not know how to get out of the realm of fantasy and face life. Others take on an **avoidance** approach as they refuse to confront the emotions that come with their deliverance process.

Program Multiples. Survivors also become program multiples or develop a split personality disorder. In my experience with deliverance sessions, victims confess that they struggle to make decisions as they experience a tug-of-war in their minds. Sometimes rape and molestation survivors know the name of the other personality living inside them. That personality can compete with the victim in the decision-making process by pushing for an opposite choice. It is even harder for survivors if the other personality is stronger because the survivor experiences another form of victimization as they fail to make their own choices independently due to the influence of another personality residing in them. During deliverance prayers, some of the multiple personalities manifest, and they disclose the age at which they entered the person, as well as what they have been doing in the life of the person. Usually, these spirits are not resistant when being cast out.

Change of body shape. In my experience in deliverance prayers, I have noticed, mostly among women survivors, bulging bellies. I have not researched the scientific explanation of it all, but I believe that some muscles are damaged in the groin area during rape, and they do not return to their original pre-rape state. As a child, I was often chided for having a big belly, but I could not explain why until I saw other rape victims with the same condition during deliverance prayers. There are foods that I could never eat for no reason, I am not sure whether they were triggers, and my digestive system has never been stable because I was whacked emotionally.

Trauma. That goes without saying. The rape experience changes the survivor completely, especially if they are young. The tendency to be hyper-vigilant can annoy those around a survivor. Yet, they are having flashbacks and triggers in some environments.

Stunted emotions For survivors who were robbed of **trust** through rape, their deliverance process goes through an episode of persuading the little girl or boy who was robbed of trust by reinforcing the fact that their inability to trust is justified because what was done to them was unfair. Survivors of rape/ molestation/sodomy tend to have their emotions frozen at the time at which the victimization happened. They may grow into an adult, but emotionally they are stuck at the age of victimization. This is why some spouses, especially husbands, sometimes lose patience with their partners because they vacillate between infantile and adult emotional expression. That confuses the partner because they do not know what response they will get from their spouse. Most of the time, the partner has no clue as to why a grown person behaves like a child. An impatient spouse can become abusive, yet the wife does not change, no matter the amount of pressure put on them to change. The survivor has no idea why they act that way. When the victim in the survivor is persuaded to trust again and release the adult to move on, some survivors experience a change in their thought processing. Usually, it is spontaneous in some survivors. The release of emotions from a little girl or boy helps the adult survivor to have a balance between their age and emotions.

Confronting emotions. In the process of deliverance, if the survivor is not resistant, the first sign of confronting their emotions is through screams. It is like pricking a sealed reservoir of panting emotions. The screams are usually accompanied by rolling on the ground as the survivor fights to regain her worth. This may be the first and only time the survivor gets in touch with their emotions, so a little drama can be expected. The important thing is for the helpers to avoid interfering with such a deeply emotional process. They can only ensure that the person does not hurt themselves.

    The screams can change into hopelessness as the person processes the pain of what happened to them. That process ends with intervention as the person helping in the deliverance assures the survivor of exhibiting the power to be brave enough to confront the perpetrator. That emotional episode has a tremendous impact on the outcome because the healing and recovery process is happening at a very deep level of the soul. Some survivors carry their pain in their faces, but after the deliverance process, there is a transformation of the facial appearance and joy through smiling. Countless survivors have changed instantly, but the process is demanding. The damage caused by rape is not a deformity of the physical body but damage to the soul. The face cannot hide what is in the soul, especially pain. Sometimes the pain is accompanied by anger too. When the soul is restored, the face reflects the change of circumstances.

Even more complicated rape cases involve women or men abused by spirits. They go through the experience of sexual intercourse with an unseen being. They cannot talk about it in most cases for fear that they will be labeled as insane. The inability to articulate what they are going through and the lack of empathy with what they are going through from those close to them worsen their condition. These women present all the characteristics of victims of rape, but their kind is spiritual- the incubus and succubus spirits are real. Consequently, such victims can be paralyzed by their pain to the point of failing to bathe during certain times of the month because the spirits zap their energy as a way of demonstrating control, inducing fear. Unlike victims of physical rape, who may not want to bathe to be unattractive to the perpetrators, victims of spiritual and sexual abuse are paralyzed to the point of failing to bathe. Sometimes they get listless. They also fail to do the normal day-to-day duties after spiritual, sexual encounters with spirits. So, their performance at work or at home declines at some times of the month. Without help encouraging them to rise, their condition can deteriorate or manifest as some form of the disease. It is sad that some of these experiences have their foundations in familial spiritual bondages. Such victims often assume awkward sleeping positions, locking up their legs when they sleep as a self-protecting measure. That can cause secondary issues related to poor blood circulation because of hypervigilance, the victim cannot afford to sleep peacefully.

It is important to note that all these negative experiences that affect individuals tend to converge on romantic relationships in one form or another. This is the fundamental purpose of this kind of bondage, That is why they are called anti-marriage spirits. It does not matter whether they were introduced into the family through rituals in the family or acts of rape. They end up disrupting the cohesion of the marriage institution.

In Zimbabwe, women were raped during the liberation war, and many of them moved on without help, mainly because those in authority did not know any better about what to do to help the many victims. Rituals in families continue unabated, thereby reinforcing existing bondages. What is needed is intervention at all levels with the understanding that some of the traditions are good at face value, but they are door openers to bondages.

False accusations
False accusations against victims are deliberate and well-planned. I lived the life of an accused among my relatives from my mother. and father's sides. To stop me from saying anything, I was always being blamed, and I ended up expending all my little energies in trying to defend myself, and prove my innocence, especially carrying a secret that I felt guilty about already; I found it hard to even think of talking about anything else if the people around me stopped accusing me. If I wanted to say anything, I would be stopped and demeaned, and the subject matter would be changed. Perpetrators and their accomplices devise ways of silencing victims. Those who hear the accusations can worsen the burden on the

victim because the victim is accused so much until the desire to defend oneself vanishes. For a victim to rise from that place of being weakened by words and sometimes beatings take a lot of courage. That is why many victims choose to keep quiet and move on. Yet, they hardly move on until the issue is addressed because their soul refuses to express a lie.

Soul ties

For young men, life is full of pressure to prove manhood, and they are trapped in a different way but still with the same result. When they sow their oats, many establish soul ties with strange women, most of whom were initiated through rape so that they live for the sole purpose of destroying men. Some women who masquerade as girls looking for pleasure are mermaids, which are after harvesting the integrity of men by taking their sperm back to the waters where mermaids live. These are common phenomena in Zimbabwe because the nation worships mermaids. Once they seduce a man, and he agrees to have sex, then they harvest the sperm and take it underwater, where it can be used in any way that destroys the man, either through poor health, mental health deterioration, self-destructive behavior, or abandoning a marriage, to mention a few effects of sexual contact with mermaids. However, the man who has a few minutes of pleasure does not understand that he has sold his legacy to the kingdom of darkness in just one act of pleasure. It is no surprise that in Zimbabwe, it is very difficult to find old money in families because the fathers sold their legacy to a strange woman through sex.

When that happens, then powers of darkness come back to people and seduce them to enter into blood covenants for prosperity. This prosperity does not only belong to the kingdom of darkness, it got into the hands of Satan because humanity did not understand the power of obeying the laws of God. Now we have people who shed blood because they want to make money, yet God stipulated in His word the principles of prosperity one should follow. People do not want the way of God, which carries in it the power to create a lasting legacy, because they want shortcuts of taking other human beings' lives. So, the cycle continues unabated until humanity humbles itself enough to ask God for forgiveness for sins so that the blood of Jesus Christ can cleanse them. When a person kills other human beings, that act is seen by God as usurping His authority because a human being acts as a god with the power to decide who should live or die. That act is a serious crime that affects the one who commits the act and those of his bloodline. When the spirit of the avenger of blood comes for revenge, innocent people are affected in many ways, like chronic diseases and mental health challenges that can lead to suicide because blood calls for blood, unless the people affected call on God for help so that the atoning blood of Jesus Christ can redeem them from destruction (Psalm 103: 4)

Another aspect of soul ties relates to casual sex. I will use one example of a young woman, highly educated, and with a promising future. She dated another educated man of her class and status. She had reservations about the relationship but eventually gave in to the man's insistence on having sex. It was a one-night stint that changed and almost took her life. The man was struggling to finish school, but she was a trailblazer. After the sexual encounter, the man suddenly cruised through school, but she struggled. She confronted the man, expressing concern over what the sexual encounter had done to her. The man was nonchalant about it. However, the woman started having strange experiences with feelings of things crawling into her head. Her health deteriorated. Unseen beings breathing and lying beside her bed became a common experience. She was being subjected to involuntary sexual encounters by unseen beings. When she requested prayer from other Christians, she said they told her that she had a spirit of death put on her. God delivered her, and she was able to move on. Here is a case of casual sex that almost cost a young woman her life and destiny. In our time, and I believe in ancient times, too, sex has been used as a weapon by both men and women to destroy the core of the life of an individual. There are mermaids among us masquerading as beautiful women, ready to bed, any ready man. This is becoming a common thing in Zimbabwe because of iniquity, but the Bible says that *"Where iniquity/sin did abound, grace did much more abound"- Romans 5:20*. All hope is not lost. The Nephilim race is not wasting time in contaminating the human race. Some men are demonized or are demonic beings who use sex as a weapon to destroy women. This writer once worked with a congregation with a man with that kind of spirit. He charmed many single mothers into sleeping with him until one of them exposed him. The Holy Spirit had told me about the man because I engaged in intercession. I heard his voice in my sleep as he confessed to what he was doing in the church regarding his inordinate relationship with women. The Holy Spirit said, *"This man who is talking is practicing spirit sex (spirit ritual sex) to gain success. To get such powers, the man slept with a corpse. The women think that he is engaging in sex with them but he is initiating them into the kingdom of darkness. After such a sexual encounter, the women cannot sustain a strong prayer life, and even their walk with God is paralyzed by that experience."*

Some parents ignorantly encourage their children to find girls to play with as an exercise regimen before they meet the right partner. They have no idea that they are abdicating their authority as the covering of the son or daughter. In the process, they leave them ravaged by a cruel world that not only takes away what the person has but preempts the future by removing all the virtues that motivate a person to win. One sexual encounter can be the death sentence that a young man or woman can be waiting for, and afterward, they can be considered as one who has fallen through the cracks and never recovered.

Premarital counseling needs to be formalized to ensure that individuals are set free before they commit to marriage. Not much emphasis is put on building such foundations before and after marriage. Many marriages are in name only as they do not exhibit any characteristic of what the institution espouses, all because of the brokenness of the partners in the institution. Strangely, most traditional counselors that I have listened to do not understand at all what they are talking about. They do not teach the youths to value their body as sacred entities. Some of the adults who are lost in terms of choices made in life were misguided by counselors, who may have deliberately, or through ignorance, misguided them into the wrong path of life. Destiny saboteurs are common in the church and families. The grace of God is needed to handle the delicate handling of raising the next generation.

It is important to incorporate marriage institution lectures for those about to graduate in cultures that have strong beliefs in the existence of the institution of marriage because relationships impact all aspects of a person's success. I have found marriage counseling, as something that is done as a routine in churches.

There is no depth of excavation of issues that have the potential to derail marriages. Sometimes, pastors who were not virgins when they married have no value in encouraging such lifestyles among their followers. They instead emphasize that a saved person is a virgin in Christ. Yes, that may be true because Jesus Christ restores our brokenness, but the loss of virginity is something to grieve and mourn for. Had the church been strong on teachings that the Bible emphasizes about the upkeep of the body, instead of spending time just focusing on the outside appearance, perhaps Roe v. Wade may not have been an issue in our time in America. Such controversies came because Biblical teachings were replaced by worldly passions and practices in the church.

Roe versus Wade is a 1973 lawsuit that famously led to the Supreme Court of the United States ruling on abortion rights. Jane Roe, an unmarried pregnant woman, filed suit for herself and others to challenge Texas abortion laws. A Texas doctor joined Roe's lawsuit, arguing that the state's abortion laws were too vague for doctors to follow.

Chapter 23

Deliverance

Deliverance is a real process in which one can be set free by the power of God from the bondage of national and family spirits and close doors that we open ourselves to by choice or ignorance. Below are some guidelines that can help in that process.
Confession of your sins and repenting is the first stage in coming back to God. Then family line sins are the next step in getting deliverance from demonic or generational bondage.

Nehemiah 1:1-10

The words of Nehemiah, the son of Hachaliah. And it came to pass in the month Chisleu, in the twentieth year, as I was in Shushan the palace,
That Hanani, one of my brethren, came, he and certain men of Judah, and I asked them concerning the Jews that had escaped, which were left of the captivity, and concerning Jerusalem.
And they said unto me, The remnants that are left of the captivity there in the province are in great affliction and reproach: the wall of Jerusalem also is broken down, and the gates thereof are burned with fire.
And it came to pass, when I heard these words, that I sat down and wept, and mourned certain days, and fasted, and prayed before the God of heaven,
And said, I beseech thee, O LORD God of heaven, the great and terrible God, that keepeth covenant and mercy for them that love him and observe his commandments: Let thine ear now be attentive, and thine eyes open, that thou mayest hear the prayer of thy servant, which I pray before thee now, day and night, for the children of Israel thy servants, and confess the sins of the children of Israel, which we have sinned against thee: both I and my father's house have sinned.
We have dealt very corruptly against thee and have not kept the commandments, nor the statutes, nor the judgments, which thou commandest thy servant Moses.

Remember, I beseech thee, the word that thou commandest thy servant, Moses, saying, If ye transgress, I will scatter you abroad among the nations:
But if ye turn unto me, and keep my commandments, and do them; though there were of you cast out unto the uttermost part of the heaven, yet will I gather them from thence, and will bring them unto the place that I have chosen to set my name there.
These are thy servants and people, whom thou hast redeemed by thy great power and by thy strong hand.
The sins of our fathers in Zimbabwe have to be acknowledged by us. We have seen a high level of idolatry in the whole country, and God is not pleased.
Many people are married to marine spirits through zvikwambo/ spirit husbands or wives, and our lives are a wreck. God is on the throne. He is watching the havoc that is going on in families. The good thing is that He hears the groaning of the prisoner and sets free those appointed to death (Psalm 102:19-20) May the Lord hear your groaning today and release you from the bondage of generations.

May the Lord, by his blood, blot out every death decree that has been made over your life according to Colossians 2:14-15, *Blotting out the handwriting of ordinances that was against us, which was contrary to us, and took it out of the way, nailing it to his cross;* **15** *And having spoiled principalities and powers, he made a shew of them openly, triumphing over them in it.*

Address the marine spirits or zvikwambo which deceive people into selling their children and relatives to the kingdom of darkness to get wealth. Divorce yourself from their hold and cancel any marriage made by your family with these spirits on your behalf.
Now speak to the anti-marriage spirits of marine worship and dispossess them of their power in Jesus' Name.
Address these spirits to release your marriage from any such bondage.
Release your children from such bondage.
Ask for refreshing times that come from the presence of the Lord on behalf of Zimbabwe, Acts 3:19 says, "*Therefore repent and return, so that your sins may be wiped away, so that times of refreshing may come from the presence of the Lord;*
Blow the trumpet in Zion according to Joel 2: 1
Blow a trumpet in Zion, And sound an alarm on My holy mountain! Let all the inhabitants of the land tremble, For the day of the LORD, is coming; Surely it is near,

Chapter 24
Testimonies

Revelation 12:11 *And they overcame him by the blood of the Lamb, and by the word of their testimony, and they loved not their lives unto the death.*

Testimony 1
This is a testimony from a man whose marriage was having problems:
"Pastor, I have a problem. My wife does not want to have sexual intercourse with me. Every night, she tells me she is too tired to have sex. This is a nightly occurrence. She drifts into sleep right by my side, and something strange happens. I hear my wife engaged in active sexual intimacy with an unseen person. I

witnessed her active response, but I did not see the male partner involved with my wife in my presence and on my bed. When I ask her about these experiences, she says that she does not know anything about what I allege is going on during her sleep.

Sometimes she changes her voice tone and speaks like a man. She challenges me, and it is like our roles in the home are reversed. For peace, I compromise, but she is insolent and refuses to make amends until I apologize. Pastor, I am tired"

In cases like the above testimony, it is difficult for the marriage to last because there are three parties in the relationship; the husband and wife, as well as a spirit husband. You can only be sure when a spirit husband is introduced into the life of a girl child or boy child. She could inherit it through her bloodline. It could be through rituals during the marriage ceremony of the parents. Another source can be the rituals done during pregnancy- kusungira, mishonga yemasuwo.

For families engaged in businesses of some sort or farming, doors to the darkness of this nature are opened in which parents seek help from herbalists for powers to succeed. The herbalist does not tell them of the side effects of the portions that he gives them. Sometimes the side effects manifest in the form of the bondage of girl children in the family. The family succeeds in their business or farming endeavors, but the herbal portions that they receive have spirits that give them the power to make the owners succeed, but these portions are backed by spiritual forces that use what is called legalism to control the family that has introduced the herbs in the family. Legalism comes from the principle of the Bible of the law of sin and trespass.

God set the tone in His word of how people should live according to the Ten Commandments. When these laws are broken, some consequences follow that are negative because there is a transgression of the law called sin. God is supposed to be the source of all prosperity. There should be no shortcuts to wealth acquisition. Shortcuts come about due to greed which opens the door to other vices. When we go to herbalists, we say God cannot care for us. Therefore, we take matters into our own hands. However, the nature of the universe is such that there is a constant battle between good and evil, darkness and light.

Human beings were created in the image of God to worship Him. All other things that we do on earth are just fringe benefits of being on earth. Still, darkness poses a threat to humanity's existence by seducing humans from total obedience to God into veering off the path set by God through seduction. Those who fall for the seduction of darkness immediately become what are called 'lawful captives'- Isaiah 49:24-25. Lawful captives are the ones that know what God says in His word, but their greed for gain or success in one way or other lures them into opening doors to the kingdom of Satan. Such an act gives them what they need from their deity, but this is done in exchange for the very soul of the people who engage in such actions. These people and their descendants become lawful captives of the kingdom of Satan. Their descendants are born under a cloud of this bondage, and they begin to carry on the dictates of the captivity entered into by their parents. When generations that follow practice the same behaviors of the previous generations, then their actions constitute what is called iniquity. Iniquity is when a person finds himself/ herself behaving just like other family members in the previous generations, engaging in destructive behavior patterns.

Testimony II
A lady reached out for deliverance, saying she had not been married. As usual, questions are asked about the family background because many women in bondage were used in farming rituals in African Purchase areas. The lady is a descendant of a farming family. As spiritual counseling went on, she pointed out that when she visited her family at the farm, she would have dreams in which a force would pull her to come to the fields at night. Then she would see her skin change as she morphed into a wolf. She said she would fight that process with the word of God, but her faith was not very strong to deal with the root of the problem. Her parents had not done much to help her. She would also have dreams of having sex with a stranger, and any romantic relationship with a man could not last long.

 Right there was a failed destiny due to the activity of **divisi**- altars that are set up using powers obtained from herbalists to boost agricultural production. These are the predicaments parents slide themselves and their generations into due to the love of power and money. Only the blood of Jesus Christ can wash all the wickedness away through repentance, renunciation, and deliverance. Knowledge of what happened in the deliverance process can be revealed by the Holy Spirit in the process of deliverance, and some people in captivity know exactly what happened to them. Still, they do not know how to get out of it and whom to talk to. This group is easy to help because they are eager to be free. Yet some other people have no clue that they are bound, and as such t but this is not true because God did not create humanity for pain. The pain came through sin in the garden of Eden when Adam and Eve were deceived by the serpent and disobeyed God.

Testimony III
A very successful lady was referred to our counseling sessions. We combine spiritual counseling and deliverance.
During the deliverance, the woman said, "I saw two mermaids leave me in fear as they ran for their lives when you started praying. One ran straight to the ocean, and one went into a water

body in Zimbabwe. They all looked at me in disbelief, wondering what had happened." The next spirit that she needed to be delivered from was to do with her dead aunt. She had been made a medium of the dead aunt by her family for many years. However, on the day of the deliverance, the supposed spirit of the aunt manifested and said," For sure, I am her aunt. She was collapsing at school and had blackouts until they accepted what I wanted from her. They formalized the process through beer brewing and carried out all formalities that made me her dwelling place" As the voice of the supposed aunt spoke, the Holy Spirit told me to ask the true spirit that was hiding behind the name of the aunt to identify itself. I did, and immediately, a male voice said, "How did you know that it's me and not her aunt?" When the victim regained consciousness, she said that even though her family had made her a medium for her aunt, one of the aunts had disputed the authenticity of the spirit that had been formally invited into the girl's life because there was no resemblance at all with the dead aunt. In other words, mischievous people in the family had, through formalities, sold the woman as a teenager to powers of darkness, claiming that it was her dead aunt. In such cases, there are elders in the family who will be in the know of what is going on, but they do not tell the truth to the parents of the child, especially the mother, that they are sacrificing the child to the powers of darkness for the sake of gain. When the spirit was exposed, it could not claim any legal grounds for possessing the woman because it was not the spirit of the dead aunt, and neither was it related to the family at all. The next step revealed more of the woman's bondage. Her siblings, who are still living, began to manifest one by one asking for forgiveness because they had all connived to sacrifice her and her children on the altar of money. One sibling had buses and pointed out that they used the woman and her children as the power to run their fleet of buses because she is intelligent and blessed. So they tapped into her virtue and that of her children to succeed. Even the sister-in-law manifested, apologizing for the wrong that she and the woman's brother had done to the victim. Next were her sisters, whom all had done many dastardly acts of harnessing her intelligence for their gain. They all explained one after another what they had done to their siblings.

In most deliverance sessions, those who counsel and deliver people who have been victimized by their families, there is a need to emphasize forgiveness because some of the confessions open doors of extreme rejection on the victim. The victim has to be counseled to understand that the nature of sin will use anyone who does not fear God, even close family members like siblings. It is heartbreaking for many to realize that Satan can use people very close to the victims. The sin of nature can manifest in any form. The only antidote to sinful nature is the confession of the name of Jesus Christ and the power of His blood.

Testimony IV
A high-ranking woman in international business came for deliverance.
She manifested the human spirits of her aunt and grandmother. Human spirits are not demonic spirits but alive people who are connected in one way or another with the victim regarding the bondage in their lives. The first human spirit of the aunt manifested laughing "Even if she brags of being in international business, we caged her success, and the husband is a confused good for nothing. It is my mother, and I did it because she thought her intelligence will lead her

somewhere. We killed her parents too. They are going nowhere."

The victim confirmed the claims made by the spirit to be true. She pointed out that her husband could not keep a job or run a business. "He ended up going back to Zimbabwe, and he is doing nothing."

We continued with the counseling, and human spirits from her husband's side manifested, and the first one was the husband's sister. "For sure, we took our brother's virtue and put it in a bottle and threw it in the ocean. We did it because we want to succeed. Don't you want us to succeed? We affected his brain, and he could not think normally. Now that his wife has caused our exposure, we are calling back the things monitoring him. "Come back, all of you. You cannot stay any longer. Release his mind and come back because there is too much fire"

We used our brother because he is the only male in our household, and our mother and all the girls sat down and agreed to sacrifice him, and yes, we are all wealthy because he is the bedrock of our success."

In dealing with human spirits, the counselor or deliverer has to emphasize telling the human spirit about the love of Jesus Christ and the hope of salvation in Jesus Christ. This is because you are talking to a real person. One cannot cast out that spirit as a demon because it's a living person who, in most cases, is related to the victim.

Chapter 25
Prayer

Father, God, I come into your presence with thanksgiving in my heart. I declare your great and mighty deeds in all the earth. You are clothed in majesty and splendor. You are awesome. I love your presence. Thank you for holding me up with your right hand of righteousness. I am strengthened by the glory from your face Jesus. I am in love with you, my Lord and King. All my worries are dissolved by your glory as I gaze into your face. My heart melts as I behold your beauty. Oh, Rose of Sharon, you are filled with majesty and wonder, all for me to behold and soak in. You walk so majestically with your sword girded by your side O Mighty One with your glory and your majesty. In your majesty, ride prosperously because of truth, humility, and righteousness. You are fairer than the sons of men. Grace is poured upon your lips. Therefore, God has blessed you forever. Your arrows are sharp in the heart of the King's enemies. The people Fall under you. Your throne, O God, is forever and ever. A scepter of righteousness is the scepter of your Kingdom. You love righteousness and hate wickedness. Therefore, God, Your God has anointed You with the oil of gladness more than Your companions. O! How I love your presence. You draw me with the smell of your garments which are scented with myrrh and cassia. I am drunk in your love, my Lord and King. (Verses mostly taken from Psalm 45)

I hallow your names, my Father God. Jehovah El Elyon- God Most High, Creator, and Possessor of Heaven and Earth. (Genesis 14: 19) Jehovah El Shaddai – God All-Powerful and All-Sufficient- *"I am thy shield and exceeding great reward" (Genesis 15: 1) Jehovah Jireh- The Lord who sees and provides (Genesis 22: 14)*

2. Repentance:

In the wretchedness of my sins, I have come, and you did not turn me away. I have not walked worthy of your statutes, but you still beckon me to come and dine with you. Forgive me for all my sins, Lord Jesus. You have brought me into your royal presence and washed me with your blood. I have failed, but you picked me up. O faithful witness, the firstborn from the dead and the ruler over the kings of the earth. You have raised me and given me life even when I did not deserve it. You have loved and washed me from my sins in Your blood. You have brought me into kingship and priesthood to your God and Father. To you be glory and dominion forever and ever. Amen. (Rev 1: 5-6) Thank you for allowing me to stand in your presence in your blood, acceptable before the Father. Thank you for making me a joint heir of the saints' inheritance.

Prayer for self:
Lord, I stand before you according to your word in Jeremiah 33:3, where you said that I should call on you and that you, in turn, will answer me and show me great and mighty things that I do not know. You also commanded in 1 Timothy 2: 1-3 that *"Therefore I exhort first of all those supplications, prayers,*

intercessions, and giving of thanks be made for all men, for kings and all who are in authority, that we may lead a quiet and peaceable life in all godliness and reverence. ³ For this is good and acceptable in the sight of God our Savior."

I stand before you, under the blood of Jesus, and present my life before you. Jesus, you are Jehovah Nissi- my Banner who ever lives to make intercession for my life before God the Father. Jesus, you are my Mercy Seat who covers me with your blood as I present my case before the throne of grace. *I was shapen in iniquity and in sin my mother bore me* (Psalm 51:5) But by grace, I stand before you to confess the wall of Jericho (character strongholds that want to hinder me from walking in the fullness of your love.) I ask your guidance on how to circle and destroy gossip, lying, cheating, envy, jealousy, narcissism, pride, rebellion against God, and wickedness, in the same manner you led the children of Israel to walk around Jericho until the walls fell. Father, God, the tradition I was raised under is making your word not affect my life. (Mark 7:13) I admit that such practices of rebellion against God and idolatry were handed down to me through culture and tradition, and they have led to bondages of character in my life. I am imprisoned in lying, envy, hatred, and bitterness, as well as unforgiveness. I saw these negative qualities in my family. I had hoped to escape them through education and sober and possibility thinking, but I realize that they are stronger than I thought and go beyond human thinking. I need your help, Lord Jesus, to destroy these strongholds. "You strongholds, I command you to fall after the manner of Jericho. I call on Jehovah Sabaoth- The Lord of Hosts (Joshua 15: 13-15) to command His host of warring angels into my condition and help me demolish the planting of the enemy out of my life as well as help me to regain my inheritance of the saints."

These strongholds will need fasting as part of the warfare to demolish them. I recommend fasting day and night to address both night and day when the doors to this captivity were opened.

Prayer for the Nation (Zimbabwe)

Father God, in the name of Jesus Christ, your Son, we come to present the nation of Zimbabwe before you. You said *Blessed is the nation whose God is the LORD, and the people he has chosen for his inheritance* (Psalm 33:12). We are your people because Jesus has washed us in His blood. Through deception and greed, our nation has been taken into captivity. We stand today as the children of Israel by the Rivers of Babylon, longing for the beauty and prosperity of a once beautiful land (Psalm 137) Our enemies taunt us and treat us as if we are nothing because we rebelled against you and all this pain and suffering has come upon us. We cannot forget Zimbabwe even though we are scattered across many lands.

Now Father, like Nehemiah, we come before you to repent of our sins according to 2 Chronicles 7:14 - *"If my people, which are called by my name, shall humble themselves, and pray, and seek my face, and turn from their wicked ways; then will I hear from heaven, and will forgive their sin, and will heal their land."*

We have sinned in practicing idolatry from generation to generation. We have called on your name in vain when our hearts have been filled with hate and envy. The nation flows with the blood of innocent people, which has come before your throne as a testimony against our ancestors, our leaders, and us. We repent and ask your forgiveness, Lord. Only you can stop the wanton killing of innocent people.

Hosea 1: 4 *And the LORD said unto him, call his name Jezreel; for yet a little while, and I will avenge the blood of Jezreel upon the house of Jehu, and will cause to cease the kingdom of the house of Israel.* Those who have shed innocent blood in families, regions, businesses, and at the national level should pay after the manner of the house of Jehu over Jezreel. Cause their kingdoms to cease as you caused the kingdom of the house of Israel to cease because of sin during the time of Hosea unless they repented.

We now present the wickedness of our nation, and we say we are sorry, Lord, for opening the doors that lead into continuous captivity-iniquity. We ask you to visit our leaders who have made covenants and pacts with darkness, and by their position, they have led the whole nation into captivity because they opened doors to evil.

Remember the wise woman in 2 Samuel 20: 22) who wailed for the pending destruction of Abel of Bethmaacah as Joab, a bloody commander, who was leading an army to destroy the city because Sheba, son of Bichri, had fled into the city. The wise woman intervened, and Joab did not destroy the city, but only Sheba, who had rebelled, was killed. 2 Samuel 20: 16 *"Then cried a wise woman out of the city, Hear, hear; say, I pray you, unto Joab, come near hither, that I may speak with thee. 17 And when he came near unto her, the woman said, Art thou Joab? And he answered I am he. Then she said unto him, Hear the words of thine handmaid. And he answered I do hear. 18 Then she spoke, saying, They were wont to speak in old times, saying, They shall surely ask counsel at Abel: and so, they ended the matter. 19 I am one of them that are peaceable and faithful in Israel: thou seekest to destroy a city and a mother in Israel: why wilt thou swallow up the inheritance of the Lord? 20 And Joab answered and said, Far be it, far be it from me, that I should swallow up or destroy. 21 The matter is not so: but a man of mount Ephraim, Sheba the son of Bichri by name, hath lifted his hand against the king, even against David: deliver him only, and I will depart from the city. And the woman said unto Joab, Behold, his head shall be thrown to thee over the wall. 22 Then the woman went unto all the people in her wisdom. And they cut off the head of Sheba, the son of Bichri, and cast it out to Joab. And he blew a trumpet, and they retired from the city, every man to his tent. And Joab returned to Jerusalem unto the king" (KJV).* In our time, Lord Jesus raised among us wise women who avert bloodshed in the nation. Women who can defeat the fury of tribalism/ethnicity, like the hatred for the tribe of Judah by Benjaminites when David became king in Israel. We pray, Lord, for perceptive intercessors that can influence decisions in their community through intercession and wisdom.

We ask for the qualities of wise women to characterize the women of our nation.
a. They have one weapon- wisdom. This is not earthly wisdom but the wisdom with which you made the worlds in I Corinthians 2: 6-10

However, we speak wisdom among those who are mature, yet not the wisdom of this age, nor of the rulers of this age, who are coming to nothing. But we speak the wisdom of God in a mystery, the hidden wisdom which God ordained before the ages for our glory, which none of the rulers of this age knew; for had they known, they would not have crucified the Lord of glory.
But as it is written:
"Eye has not seen, nor ear heard, nor have entered into the heart of man, the things which God has prepared for those who love Him."
But God has revealed them to us through His Spirit. For the Spirit searches all things, yes, and the deep things of God.

The wise women are not afraid: they can confront an angry and determined army commander who is used to shedding innocent blood to stop him. Lord, you know how Zimbabwe flows with innocent blood from generations of war and unending road carnages. Women who look the enemy in the face and refrain from fear- ask for the enemy's identity to confirm if they are addressing the right target because they do not want their intercession to be misdirected.

c. We pray for women like Esther who are prepared to perish to bring about change in their cities and nation. Raise such women, Lord.

Lord, our case in Zimbabwe is not about rebellion like in the case of Sheba, the son of Bichri, it is one of oppression of the weak by those who wield power. Only your intervention will bring order to Zimbabwe.

d. We confess that blood has been shed from time immemorial. We live with ethnic groups that have been silenced for generations to assert the hegemony of the strong. You said in your words, *"If the foundation is destroyed, what can the righteous do" (Psalm 11: 3)* The foundations of the nation are distorted by our worship of deities that you forbade your people to worship, and as a result, there is no stability from generation to generation. We need your mercy, Lord!!

e. Worshiping patterns have been far removed from the true and living God to gods who cannot save, and we have provoked your anger over the generations. We revere Mulimo at Njelele as supreme over Jehovah Sabaoth. As a result, we have been stricken by all kinds of plagues from generation to generation, yet we still grope in darkness without humbling ourselves to seek a godly solution.

f. Raise a remnant that will cause restoration of this nation to the worship of one true God and cause the tribes to engage in identification repentance so that we may hear the voice of rejoicing again. We pray that the bride and bridegroom will rejoice to have a godly union that is not interfered with by marine spirits that the nation has been dedicated to. As we stand in the gap, we are ashamed of the number of marriages that have not brought happiness to our nation because marine influence has been given an upper hand. Our babies are dedicated to these spirits at birth. Thereby ruining their chances of independently choosing spouses and having holy marriages because of disruptions from marine influences.

g. We pray to you, heavenly Father, that you visit the foundations of Zimbabwe and shake all the false foundations that have masqueraded as the real ones over the years. Visit us in your splendor the places that we have designated as sacred and judge them according to your righteous decrees so that that which has not been ordained by you may fall after the manner of the idol of Dagon before the Ark of the Covenant of the Living God in Philistia. 1

Samuel 5: 1-5 *"Then the Philistines took the ark of God and brought it from Ebenezer to Ashdod. When the Philistines took the ark of God, they brought it into the temple of Dagon and set it by Dagon. And when the people of Ashdod arose early in the morning, there was Dagon, fallen on its face to the earth before the ark of the Lord. So, they took Dagon and set it in its place again. And when they arose early the next morning, there was Dagon, fallen on its face to the ground before the ark of the Lord. The head of Dagon and both the palms of its hands were broken off on the threshold; only Dagon's torso was left of it. Therefore, neither the priests of Dagon nor any who come into Dagon's house tread on the threshold of Dagon in Ashdod to this day."*

Chapter 26
A call for African Continental Repentance

As I worked in the mission field of North America, I was amazed by African spiritual influence in the north and central America societies. I realized that some of the Voodoo, Palo- Mayombe, and Santeria types of witchcraft all have their origin from the African continent. Slavery transported many worship practices from the African continent to the lands of bondage.

Voodoo is defined as a form of religious witchcraft. It is a spiritual, ancestor-based religion that originated in West Africa and is practiced primarily in **Haiti**. The word "voodoo" originated around 1850 in Louisiana, likely from the French word "voudou" or perhaps from the West African word "vodu." It is also spelled "vodou," "vodun," and "voudou".

Palo Mayombe has its origin in Congo.

It is an ancient diaspora religion brought to Cuba by Congolese slaves. From Cuba, it spread throughout the Caribbean to the Dominican Republic, Colombia, Venezuela, and later to the US. It's called Palo Mayombe, and its dark rituals involving human and animal remains and even grave robbing are practiced in extreme secrecy and were transported to Cuba by slaves. It is regarded as the evil twin of Santeria because of the darkness associated with it.

Santería, also known as Regla de Ocha, Regla Lucumí, or Lucumí, is an African diasporic religion that developed in Cuba during the late 19th century. It arose through syncretism between the traditional Yoruba religion of West Africa, the Roman Catholic form of Christianity, and Spiritism.

Santeria in Spanish means "The Way of the Saints." While Regla de Ocha, Regla means *The way of the Orishas* (Yoruba deities)

From Ancient Egypt, Africa has projected a spiritual belief system that has gained worldwide acclaim. African traditional practices have exerted influence that has outlived slavery throughout the lands that practiced slavery. If a comparison is to be made between the influence and impact of African tradition drawing from the examples cited above, then the influence of traditional or diaspora religion has consolidated itself more as part of the daily life in the Americas. In that case, the African influence is felt in the Americas and Hispania in greater measure.

 This is not in any way to demean the pain of slavery as a dark era of history. The flip side of slavery is that African religious practices forever changed the lands that engaged in or were destinations of slavery. Why is mentioning African spiritual influence in the Americas important? It is so that African descendants can face the dark side of their belief systems and practices and repent for exerting such a negative influence on other cultures. Not all slaves converted to Christianity. Many continued to hold on to their religion, which no one should dispute because it was and still is, their right. However, there should be an admission by Africans that some of the practices are not pleasing to God and brought a dark influence on other cultures. If we do not face our weaknesses as a race, we continue to label ourselves as victims of other races instead of repenting for our sins before God which we continue to label as tradition. Before God, we have transgressed his laws for generations. This does not minimize the effect of enslavement. It is a call to look into ourselves, and correct the weaknesses that we have not had time to look into because of the pressures of life. Both of them make their practitioners liable to be judged by God. Asking God for forgiveness is important for posterity because our belief systems have been contrary to the laws of God, and that is called **sin.**

In other words, the altars of idolatry and rebellion against God in Africa exert their influence over many continents. When voodoo, santeria, and Palo Mayombe practitioners die without knowing God, their blood is required from the hands of the seed of Africa. This is a reality that we cannot shout ourselves out of. We must repent before the God of heaven because our sin is great.

It is, therefore, no surprise that those who are on the continent continue in ways that do not please God which are dubbed tradition. If God was to ask Africa for reparations for the spiritual damage it has done to other nations through religious influence, how much would the cost be? How much would Africa pay the God of Heaven? I am not engaging in self-deprecation but genuinely expressing the need for my race to put its house in order.

Rituals like rape, incest, sodomy, and human sacrifice signify that witchcraft is practiced unabatedly. Missionaries brought the gospel as a mandate from God because He loves Africa. The onus is on the continent to choose whether to remain the exporter of practices that are contrary to the God of Heaven or to look within the continent and make a decision to ask for mercy. Today, people go to church on Sunday, but they practice witchcraft on the side. And to such, Jesus will say one day, soon, according to *Matthew* 7: 21-23, *"Not everyone who says to me, 'Lord, Lord,' will enter the kingdom of heaven, but the one who does the will of my Father who is in heaven. 22 On that day, many will say to me, 'Lord, Lord, did we not prophesy in your name, and cast out demons in your name, and do many mighty works in your name?' 23 And then will I declare to them, 'I never knew you; depart from me, you workers of lawlessness.'*

Chapter 27
Signs of apostasy/ the great falling away

Apostacy is the abandonment or renunciation of a religious or political belief. There is great concern that young people are turning away from God *en mass*. Lately, even adults are abandoning their belief in Christ Jesus too. On the other hand, the emphasis on identity has been hyped up. Meaning that an individual or self is taking center stage. The propping up of self is associated with a call to return to traditional beliefs and practices. For some reason, different nationalities seem to have woken up to the power of national or individual identity. This is expressed in many forms. Governments must recognize different ethnic groupings for political survival or equitable resource distribution. Strangely, any time that emphasis is put on tradition, faith in

Jesus Christ begins to wane. People are eager to establish their proper ancestry so that they can imitate the lifestyle of their ancestors. Even wars are being fought over issues of identity the world over. However, Jesus Christ addressed the issue of tradition unequivocally. The Gospel according to Saint Mark Chapter 7, from verse 5 says,

⁵ Then the Pharisees and scribes asked him, Why walk not thy disciples according to the tradition of the elders, but eat bread with unwashen hands?
⁶ He answered and said unto them, Well hath Esaias prophesied of you hypocrites, as it is written, This people honoureth me with their lips, but their heart is far from me.
⁷ Howbeit in vain do they worship me, teaching for doctrines the commandments of men.
⁸ For laying aside the commandment of God, ye hold the tradition of men, as the washing of pots and cups: and many other such like things ye do.
⁹ And he said unto them, Full well ye reject the commandment of God, that ye may keep your own tradition.
¹⁰ For Moses said, Honour thy father and thy mother; and, Whoso curseth father or mother, let him die the death:

[11] But ye say, If a man shall say to his father or mother, It is Corban, that is to say, a gift, by whatsoever thou mightest be profited by me; he shall be free.
[12] And ye suffer him no more to do ought for his father or his mother;

[13] Making the word of God of none effect through your tradition, which ye have delivered: and many such like things do ye.

      The word of God talks about apostasy as a precursor to the revealing of the son of perdition before Jesus Christ returns. The return to tradition, and the ways of the fathers is not a fad, but a predicted period in the Bible. 2 Thessalonians 2, points out, *Now we beseech you, brethren, by the coming of our Lord Jesus Christ, and by our gathering together unto him,*
***2** That ye be not soon shaken in mind, or be troubled, neither by spirit, nor by word, nor by letter as from us, as that the day of Christ is at hand.*
***3** Let no man deceive you by any means: for that day shall not come, except there come a falling away first, and that man of sin be revealed, the son of perdition;*
***4** Who opposeth and exalteth himself above all that is called God, or that is worshipped; so that he as God sitteth in the temple of God, shewing himself that he is God.*

All of a sudden people find church abhorrent. There is confusion in the church itself, just like there is commotion in the governmental systems of this world. Instead of running to seek God as some people did in the past, many go to clairvoyants, soothsayers, and palm readers for solutions. The reason is that if people are clean before God, following His ways then the Antichrist cannot find a sufficiently defiled world for him to manifest. So, he is seducing humanity slowly into rebellion against God by making choices that are forbidden by God. The more people rebel, the more they defile themselves, and the more they create a suitable environment for the prevalence of evil. This is why I refer to my rape experiences as defilement because the same spirit of the antichrist has been working to stop those of us who have a calling of God from fulfilling it by desecrating us from a young age. It does not matter how the abuse was done; the end result was to destroy the foundation in order to stop the fulfillment of God's plan on earth.

Lately, young girls are being seduced by mermaid spirits, being recruited as wives of spirits or human agents of those that live under the waters. The allurements of prosperity in an environment of competition cause many young people to sell their souls to the devil, and many are doomed eternally after making such choices. And yet others find grace through Jesus Christ to escape from eternal damnation through salvation. Young people need to know that all that glitters is not gold. It is important to recognize that some of the poverty that people experience is a trap to lure them into the snare of evil. The unwise will sell their whole destiny in order to gain temporary relief from poverty, but they will spend an eternity in hell. This is why Jesus Christ beckons us to come to Him for rest. Jesus Christ even pointed out that in the world, we will suffer tribulation but we should rejoice because He has overcome the world- John 16:33. Hope for humanity is found in Christ because on our own we cannot fight the battles in the world and win, because Satan has designed it in such a way that humanity should be seduced into sinning against God, but Jesus Christ has overcome such powers.

 It is important to turn down people and organizations that ask you to join them promising opportunities, and wealth if only you pledge to be a member or even to go through rituals. There is no other God other than Jesus Christ, and your allegiance should be to Him alone. For those who have already pledged your lives, you can renounce it by asking the blood of Jesus Christ to redeem you.

Chapter 28
Conclusion

The Bible points out that the love of money is the root of all evil.
Greed has led to untold suffering throughout the ages. It is not only in Zimbabwe where people sell themselves to the kingdom of darkness for gain and power in this life. If it can make them gain more of what they are looking for, they can devalue relations and turn on the family to destroy them for gain.
My journey has been hard. I lived for many years, not knowing whether I would see the next day. A new day is a gift that we can never take for granted. I experienced the value of life, the power of love, and forgiveness. This is because some of the sufferings that we go

through are not always about us, so we get labeled victims or survivors. Unfortunately, humanity will never sympathize with a pain they have never experienced. I had to go through it to write about what I witnessed and experienced firsthand. There was no guarantee that I would live through that season of trial, but the grace of God enabled me to come out alive. I experienced deliverance from the Holy Spirit. Many pastors had no clue of what I was going through because some of them were wrapped in that system.

    The nature of a trial is that the person experiencing it should not depend on their understanding because most encounters do not make sense. If one wants to consult those around him or her, the mission can be aborted because the path is designed for one, and cramming people in the season of one's battle with their destiny can mess up the mission. I was constantly presented with opportunities in which I could choose to quit, and it would have made sense to do so. I choose not to do so by the grace of God. I fell many times because I did not understand the magnitude of the battle before me. I find it hard to blame struggling Christians because I endured many challenges in my walk.

I had to choose to leave my children for a decade. I had to stay in places where I was not welcome because God had said that I should be there. The deliverance process does not make sense at all when God is doing it. It is those who choose to look to Christ who make it out of that dark tunnel. I met an Indian pastor called Prince Thomas in 2014, and he said, "Do you know that many people who went through the path that you traveled did not come out alive? You made it alive because of the favor of God upon your life. You have the favor of Esther of the Bible. When God raised Esther, many were astonished. God will raise you to a place of influence in society because He favors you" Pastor Thomas was very specific about what God was going to do with my life in the future. Why is it important to mention such things? It is so that you who read this book to the end may know that for sure, *"Weeping may endure for a night, but joy comes in the morning"*- Psalm 30:5

Ridicule is part of the game. Fellow ministers, ordinary people, and family laughed at me to scorn. It was in those moments that I knew that only God is a Mighty Fortress and a Bulwark that never fails. There was a time when I was just alone, with no money in my pocket yet, I had more than one college degree that could get me out of my bind, but because God had not told me to make a move, I stayed put. God was not making me a zombie; it was a time of disciplined training.

Some people can never do God's will if their family surrounds them. Most of the time, the call of God comes with a very painful separation from family. Joseph in the bible is an example. They even faked his death and forgot about him. Many of us have been taught about a call of God that makes heroes out of us, but even Christ the Son of God had to go through suffering to lead by example in Hebrews 5: 7-10

7 Who in the days of his flesh, when he had offered up prayers and supplications with strong crying and tears unto him that was able to save him from death, and was heard in that he feared;

8 Though he were a Son, yet learned he obedience by the things which he suffered;

9 And being made perfect, he became the author of eternal salvation unto all them that obey him;

10 Called of God a high priest after the order of Melchizedek.

There are heights of glory we may never attain until we have allowed God to have His way without any objection. In Zimbabwe, God is demonstrating that if He can shame a family system that wants to devour its members, then He will utterly destroy the Njelele- Nehanda system and restore the nation to the way that He wants it to be. He delivered me, and I am not the only one, and all those people who have been delivered are expected to be productive by causing others to be set free through the power of God.

It is sad to see the level of ignorance of the level of bondage that comes with the worship of the Njelele- Nehanda alliance. Not all people are ignorant of what is going on, though. Some citizens have prospered from bowing down to that alliance through evil covenants. The activities that characterize their worship of this alliance suck innocent people into destructions ranging from rape, fatal accidents, molestation through sodomy, and incest, human ritual sacrifice for abundant harvests, as well as to strengthen reins of power. I suffered greatly at the hands of such endeavors by my own family for many years.

    Hope for change comes through understanding that the battle between the kingdom of God and Satan cannot be wished away. It is an existential issue. One is either a member of one or the other. That is how the universe is made up. When one understands the prudence of submitting to God through Jesus Christ, God takes it upon Himself to protect the person. This is not something new. Neither is it a fad. There is a real war going on for the control of the human soul. The wise seek help from God, and the unwise make wild goose chases of material things without eternal value. From my interactions with my father, I realized the importance of forgiveness. As I listened to him talk about his upbringing, I realized that we had so much in common in terms of our experiences. Still, one was hardened into bitterness by their experiences, and the other was crushed by their experiences but learned forgiveness in the process through the mercies of God. My father lost his mother while he was very young. He grew up in an abusive household. He was bitter towards women because of his experiences. He developed an attitude of using women as objects of pleasure. The truth is that no one had taught him how to relate to women, so he followed what he thought was the best way to do it. He was a hardened man. Most, if not all, the women who related to him, did it for romantic reasons, but I do not think my father knew what love was.

Even with his wife, my father was rough in the early days of my stay with him, but he changed for the better with time. The Holy Spirit told me that when I showed my father, unconditional love, he learned for the first time in his life to receive love from a genuine female. I remember correcting him when I noticed he was fighting with his wife. Of course, I knew I was the reason for the fights, but I chose to correct my father so he would not act irresponsibly. He seemed to receive my corrections like a little boy, which made me wonder why? He was hearing the voice of correction from a female who neither demeaned nor condemned him, and he seemed to love it.

When the Holy Spirit told me to start withdrawing from the family, He also mentioned that both my father and I had been healed. I did not think my father needed any healing, but he did. He was the type of person who would referee fights between his sons and derive so much joy from seeing his children fighting. Whenever his wife went away on business, he would call the boys to challenge and fight each other. To me, that was a very sad demonstration of fatherhood. He even sowed seeds of discord between me and my sister. I do not know what he told my sister, but after some discussions with her, my father came to me and said, "When I die, the person to watch for is your sister because she will give you problems because her heart towards you is not right." If my sister was evil, why would she have to wait for him to die before she manifested her hatred? It appeared to be something programmed that would manifest in a particular season. I never enjoyed a healthy relationship with my sister. I realized that in my father's bitterness, it was a very small thing to get rid of pregnancy no matter what stage it was, as he had tried to when my mother was carrying me.

It was very clear to me that when someone is a victim, they will inadvertently victimize someone throughout their life because, in some cases, victims victimize. From his sorrow, abandonment, and abuse as a child, he also became an abuser. He was applying learned behavior from his childhood, only that he made it a combination of occultism and vindictiveness. With that understanding, I could forgive him and all the other family members.

Women are the mothers of a nation. When women are weakened in any way, that nation is weakened for generations. As I labor in deliverance sessions, I encounter heart-rending stories of children being abused by their parents. Parents use fear-mongering on their children to control their lives, money, and whom they should marry. Many Zimbabwean parents are self-serving in all they do for their children. Love does not seem to be the reason. I was saddened by the story of a woman who referred to one of her daughters as her "retirement." The mother would disqualify every suitor that dates her daughter because the mother's mind was made up that her daughter is not going to marry. Having children out of wedlock was a plausible option for the mother, but marriage for her daughter was out of the question. The daughter had no idea what her mother was up to. She confided in her and believed that her mother was her pillar of support. Can you imagine the heartbreak that the girl will suffer when she realizes that her mother is the stumbling block to her progress? This practice is a form of witchcraft because there is no human being with the power to alter the course of the life of another person created by God. This is very common in Zimbabwe. God cannot ignore the cry of the innocents who are subjected to pain and misery by those who are supposed to love them. God will judge the perpetrators, whether at the individual or national level.

The Njelele- Nehanda Alliance exercises its control through churches too. It blends itself with church agendas and appears to be a real form of worship of the Living God just like Santeria. The culture of respect based on our tradition appears wonderful at face value, but the oppression attached to the culture also infiltrates the churches if allowed to. Many people in Zimbabwean churches are oppressed by a religious spirit. Once that is achieved, then the ruling spirits of the nation exercise their dominion over the affairs of the house of God.

    The danger of religious spirits is that they increase the bondage of the people who have come to the house of God for deliverance. This can happen in a church with or without the knowledge of the leadership, and this would be a spirit of witchcraft that seeks to control and changes the course of the vision of the church. Very often, such spirits are identified and rooted up. The presence of God can be so strong that no evil can stand in such a place. However, churches that make it so hard for people to live freely in the church because of challenging rules cause people to hide their weaknesses and pretend to be believers. Once that happens, a religious spirit then oppresses the people. One of the signs of the presence of this spirit is sexual immorality or perversion. Here is the reason. When we subject ourselves to a religious spirit, we weaken the connection of our fellowship with God. That act alone is spiritual prostitution. We play the harlot as believers when we go with another spirit instead of the Spirit of Christ. Hosea 4:12 *My people ask counsel at their stocks, and their staff declare unto them: for the spirit of whoredoms hath caused them to err, and they have gone a whoring from under their God.* Sexual immorality in a church is mostly a sign that the spirit of error has entered the body of believers. It has to be dealt with through repentance. It uses legalism to deny people the liberty that they have in Christ.

    Church becomes a chore and not a place of love and fellowship. Jesus said that *"By their fruit, you shall know them"* Matthew 7: 20. Since our culture does not encourage challenging authority, church members struggle to deal with an issue of error for a long time before they muster up the courage to address it. Half the time, church members do not question leadership, and the enemy uses that avenue to seduce and deceive people into falling in line with a wrong doctrine. The moment that they agree with something that is not in line with the word of God, gradually, many of them succumb to sexual immorality. This is not because they are bad people but because their alignment with a wrong belief system causes them to veer off the path of God. In doing so, they meet other lovers. A religious spirit in a body of believers always manifests in the form of the physical act of sexual immorality because what happens in the spirit manifests physically.

Let us all be ready for the return of Jesus Christ. He is coming soon.

Revelation 21:1-11

And I saw a new heaven and a new earth: for the first heaven and the first earth were passed away; and there was no more sea.

2 And I John saw the holy city, new Jerusalem, coming down from God out of heaven, prepared as a bride adorned for her husband.

3 And I heard a great voice out of heaven saying, Behold, the tabernacle of God is with men, and he will dwell with them, and they shall be his people, and God himself shall be with them, and be their God.

4 And God shall wipe away all tears from their eyes; and there shall be no more death, neither sorrow, nor crying, neither shall there be any more pain: for the former things are passed away.

⁵ And he that sat upon the throne said, Behold, I make all things new. And he said unto me, Write: for these words are true and faithful.

⁶ And he said unto me, It is done. I am Alpha and Omega, the beginning and the end. I will give unto him that is athirst of the fountain of the water of life freely.

⁷ He that overcometh shall inherit all things; and I will be his God, and he shall be my son.

⁸ But the fearful, and unbelieving, and the abominable, and murderers, and whoremongers, and sorcerers, and idolaters, and all liars, shall have their part in the lake which burneth with fire and brimstone: which is the second death.

⁹ And there came unto me one of the seven angels which had the seven vials full of the seven last plagues, and talked with me, saying, Come hither, I will shew thee the bride, the Lamb's wife.

¹⁰ And he carried me away in the spirit to a great and high mountain, and shewed me that great city, the holy Jerusalem, descending out of heaven from God,

¹¹ Having the glory of God: and her light was like unto a stone most precious, even like a jasper stone, clear as crystal;

Sources

Ayodele, Bode (2009) *The Marine Kingdom: Deliverance from Spirit Husband and Spirit Wife* Christian Living http://www.faithwriters.com/article-details.php?id=96267

Chigwedere, Aeneas (1980) *From Mutapa to Rhodes* Macmillan

Chivaura, Gukwe Vimbai (2014, April 16) Njelele: Spiritual Centre for Murenga founder ancestor of Zimbabwe *The Patriot* ; Old posts www.thepatriot.co.zw

Custer, Shawn. (2022, March, 15) *Voodoo Religion Origins, History, & Beliefs | What is*

Voodoo? History of Major World Religions Study Guide/ Western Religions
https://study.com/learn/lesson/voodoo-religions-origins-history-beliefs.html

Dictionary.com
https://www.dictionary.com/browse/sadomasochist

Enoch, (2013)*The Book of Enoch, Prophet*, Wisdom Books, From- The Apocrypha and Pseudepigrapha of The Old Testament

Giardino, Neil. (2015, May 13) *The Traditions of Palo Mayombe* Pavement Pieces
https://pavementpieces.com/traditions-of-palo-mayombe/

Haasbroek, Jan. *Nduri dzenhango dzemuZimbabwe.* Mambo Press; Gweru; 1980.

Murphy, Joseph, M. *Santeria* Britannica
https://www.britannica.com/topic/Santeria

Mitinhima, Jinda (2016, January 24) Nyakasikana, the unspoken mermaid spirit of Nzunza

Ndhlovu, Mandhla, (20 Mar, 2019) *Bulawayo 24*

https://bulawayo24.com/news/national/158631

Nzenza, Sekai Ph. D. (2016,March 23) Easter time: Memories of Njelele, Mabweadziva *The Herald: Features and Opinions*

https://images.search.yahoo.com/search/images;_ylt=Awr9JnFthvxg07cA.y9XNyoA;_ylu=Y29sbwNncTEEcG9zAzMEdnRpZAMEc2VjA3Nj?p=where+is+Cecil+John+Rhodes%27s+grave+located&fr=mcafee

https://bible.knowing-jesus.com/topics/Incest#thematic_title_23691
Sumrall, Lester. (1995) *Pioneers of Faith* Harrison House, Tulsa, Oklahoma

Karanganda TV for chief innauguartion

https://images.search.yahoo.com/search/images;_ylt=Awr9JnFthvxg07cA.y9XNyoA;_ylu=Y29sbwNncTEEcG9zAzMEdnRpZAMEc2VjA3Nj?p=where+is+Cecil+John+Rhodes%27s+grave+located&fr=mcafee
 https://bible.knowing-jesus.com/topics/Incest

Ndhlovu, Bruce, (12 December, 2021) Cont Mhlanga, and the endless search for King Lobengula's grave, *Entertainment,* The Sunday News https://www.sundaynews.co.zw/watch-cont-mhlanga-and-the-endless-search-for-king-lobengulas-grave/

Temme, Laura, Esq. *Reviewed by Marshall, Ally Esq. (June 30, 2022) Roe v. Wade Case Summary: What You Need to Know* Findlaw, https://supreme.findlaw.com/supreme-court-insights/roe-v--wade-case-summary--what-you-need-to-know.html

Webster, Merriam (1828) *Dictionary* https://www.merriam-webster.com/dictionary/pentagram

All scripture references are from The King James Version and The New American Standard Version.